EVERYTHING WE NEED

Bible Study Notes on
The Epistle to the Ephesians

**Titles in the
Bible Study Notes Series**

Everything We Need: Ephesians
Contending for the Faith: Jude

Everything We Need

*Bible Study Notes on
The Epistle to the Ephesians*

Glen A. Blanscet

Copyright © 2020 by Glen A. Blanscet
Carrollton, Texas // www.glenblanscet.com

Cover Design by Georgia Rutherford
Author Photo by Becky Blanscet

All rights reserved. No part of this book may be used or reproduced by any means, graphic, electronic, or mechanical, including photocopying, recording, taping, or by any information storage retrieval system without the written permission of the author except in the case of brief quotations embodied in critical articles and reviews.

Because of the dynamic nature of the Internet, any web addresses or links contained in this book may have changed since publication and may no longer be valid.

Printed in the United States of America

ISBN: 978-1-7344578-2-7 (paperback)
ISBN: 978-1-7344578-3-4 (e-book)
Library of Congress Control Number: 2020907689

Version date: July 2020

All Scripture quotations, unless otherwise indicated, are taken from the Holy Bible, New International Version®, NIV®. Copyright ©1973, 1978, 1984, 2011 by Biblica, Inc.™ Used by permission of Zondervan. All rights reserved worldwide. www.zondervan.com. The "NIV" and "New International Version" are trademarks registered in the United States Patent and Trademark Office by Biblica, Inc.™

Scripture quotations marked "CSB" are taken from the Christian Standard Bible®, Copyright © 2017 by Holman Bible Publishers. Used by permission. Christian Standard Bible®, and CSB® are federally registered trademarks of Holman Bible Publishers.

Scripture quotations marked "ESV" are taken from The Holy Bible, English Standard Version® (ESV®) Copyright © 2001 by Crossway, a publishing ministry of Good News Publishers. Used by permission. All rights reserved. ESV Text Edition: 2016.

Scripture quotations marked "HCSB" are taken from the Holman Christian Standard Bible®, Copyright © 1999, 2000, 2002, 2003 by Holman Bible Publishers. Used by permission. Holman Christian Standard Bible®, Holman CSB®, and HCSB® are federally registered trademarks of Holman Bible Publishers.

Scriptures marked "NASB" are taken from the NEW AMERICAN STANDARD® (NASB), Copyright © 1960, 1962, 1963, 1968, 1971, 1972, 1973, 1975, 1977, 1995 by The Lockman Foundation. Used by permission.

Some quotations have been taken from *Ephesians: An Ironside Expository Commentary,* © 2007 by H.A. Ironside. Published by Kregel Publications, Grand Rapids, MI. Used by permission of the publisher. All rights reserved.

Some quotations have been taken from the *Life Application Bible Commentary: Ephesians* by Bruce B. Barton, et al. Copyright © 1996. Used by permission of Tyndale House Publishers, a Division of Tyndale House Ministries. All rights reserved.

Praise be to the God and Father of our Lord Jesus Christ,

who has blessed us in the heavenly realms with

every spiritual blessing in Christ.

-- Ephesians 1:3

Table of Contents

Introduction xi

Outline of the Epistle to the Ephesians xv

Chapter I	Introduction to the Epistle to the Ephesians (Ephesians 1:1-2) 1	
Chapter II	Every Spiritual Blessing in Christ (Ephesians 1:3-14) 11	
Chapter III	Paul's Prayer for Our Enlightenment (Ephesians 1:15-23) 31	
Chapter IV	From Death to Life (Ephesians 2:1-10) 41	
Chapter V	Jesus's Peace Mission (Ephesians 2:11-22) 51	
Chapter VI	Paul's Prayer for Power (Ephesians 3:1-21) 61	
Chapter VII	Living in Unity (Ephesians 4:1-16) 79	
Chapter VIII	Living in Purity (Ephesians 4:17-5:2) 95	
Chapter IX	Living as Children of Light (Ephesians 5:3-21) 109	

Chapter X	Living in Mutual Submission (Ephesians 5:21-6:9)	121
Chapter XI	Living with Strength and Courage (Ephesians 6:10-20)	137
Chapter XII	Closing Statements (Ephesians 6:21-24)	149

Notes	153
Sources Cited	175
Also by the Author	181

Introduction

MANY CHRISTIAN THEOLOGIANS consider Paul's letter to the Ephesians one of the most significant and influential documents in Christendom.[1] It covers all of the significant theological themes addressed by Paul in his other letters, such as justification by faith, the doctrine of the church, the role of the Holy Spirit, and the Christian lifestyle. In addition, it has been quoted frequently and used considerably in religious liturgy and readings throughout Christian history, second only to Romans and possibly Psalms and the Gospel of John.[2]

Some people refer to the book of Ephesians as a spiritual treasure trove for Christians because it speaks of the great riches and inheritances Christians have as a result of their relationship with Jesus Christ.[3] It frequently describes the spiritual riches of believers by contrasting their former lives as nonbelievers with their new lives in Christ, which highlights the focus and theme of this particular Bible study. The title "Everything We Need" emphasizes the voluminous blessings and riches that belong to all followers of Jesus Christ and alludes to the fact that we possess all of the resources necessary to live a lifestyle consistent with those blessings and riches.

The significance of the message of Ephesians becomes more apparent when we consider the number of people who attempt to find meaning and identity through the advice given in the voluminous self-help books and conferences available today.

Most of these resources never consider God or His Word as the means for finding our identity or self-worth. People are being led to look only to themselves in order to find meaning in life, and, as a result, they miss it completely. The Christian, however, knows that a relationship with Christ is the source of true meaning and self-worth. That truth is the focus of Paul's letter to the Ephesians, in which he guides believers to understand their position in Christ and the incredible possessions they have because of their relationship with Him.

The stories of many Christians today, however, are similar to that of Hetty Green, an American businesswoman of the late

1800s who made a fortune on Wall Street and became the richest woman and one of the richest persons in America at the time. She was a savvy financier who managed her own funds and investments into a $100 million estate by the time she died in 1916.

Despite her vast wealth, Hetty Green was also considered America's greatest miser.[4] She once carried a bag with several hundred thousand dollars' worth of securities to her bank after walking from her home all the way to downtown New York City. Her banker, John J. Cisco, chastised her for taking such a risk of being attacked and robbed on the streets and asked her why she did not ride a carriage downtown. Hetty replied, "You may be able to ride in cabs, Cisco, but I can't afford it."[5]

Other stories about Hetty Green tell of her eating cold oatmeal to save money from heating it, living in poor conditions, and dressing her children in used clothing. The most notorious story about her stinginess occurred when her teenage son broke his leg in an accident. She took him to a free clinic in the city, but when the doctor recognized her and demanded payment anyway, she refused to let the doctor treat her son, deciding that the leg would heal on its own with her home treatments. In time, the boy's leg worsened, became gangrenous, and had to be amputated.[6]

Hetty Green had unimaginable wealth at her disposal but chose to live like a pauper. Similarly, Christians have unlimited spiritual wealth at their disposal. Paul told the Ephesians we have "every spiritual blessing in Christ." In other words, when we receive Jesus Christ as our Savior and Lord, we also receive all of the spiritual blessings God offers and everything we need in order to live life as God intends. Yet many still choose to live defeated, empty lives as though they were spiritual paupers. The letter to the Ephesians is a clarion call to all believers to live their lives in a manner that is consistent with who we are and what we possess in Jesus Christ.

* * * * *

This book contains the notes I developed in my studies and preparation to teach the Book of Ephesians. My hope is that these notes will help you as you prepare to teach this important letter to others or as you read the letter for your own personal devotions. It is also my prayer that the notes will guide you to a fuller understanding of the message of Ephesians and its application in your own life.

Glen A. Blanscet
www.glenblanscet.com

Outline of
The Epistle to the Ephesians

I. Ephesians 1: 1-2 – Introduction and Background

II. Ephesians 1:3-14 – Every Spiritual Blessing in Christ
   A. Praise to God (1:3)
   B. The Blessings of God the Father (1:4-6)
      1. Chosen (1:4)
      2. Adopted (1:5)
      3. Graced (1:6)
   C. The Blessings of Jesus Christ (1:7-13a)
      1. Redeemed (1:7-8)
      2. Informed (1:9-10)
      3. Included (1:11-13a)
   D. The Blessings of the Holy Spirit (1:13b-14)
      1. Sealed (1:13b)
      2. Guaranteed (1:14)

III. Ephesians 1:15-23 – Paul's Prayer for Our Enlightenment
   A. The Reasons for Paul's Gratitude (1:15-16)
   B. The Content of Paul's Prayer (1:17-23)
      1. Wisdom and Revelation (1:17)
      2. Enlightenment (1:18-23)
         a. Of Our Hope (1:18a)
         b. Of Our Riches (1:18b)
         c. Of Our Power (1:19-23)

IV. Ephesians 2:1-10 – From Death to Life
- A. What We Once Were (2:1-3)
    1. Dead (2:1)
    2. Enslaved to Evil (2:2-3a)
    3. Objects of God's Wrath (2:3b)
- B. What We Have Become (2:4-10)
    1. Brought to Life (2:4-6)
    2. Given a Purpose (2:7-10)

V. Ephesians 2:11-22 – Jesus's Peace Mission
- A. Our Need for Reconciliation (2:11-12)
- B. Christ's Work of Reconciliation (2:13-18)
- C. The Results of Reconciliation (2:19-22)

VI. Ephesians 3:1-21 – Paul's Prayer for Power
- A. Paul, the Prisoner of Christ (3:1)
- B. Paul, the Steward of God's Mystery (3:2-7)
- C. Paul, the Servant of the Gospel Message (3:8-13)
- D. The Reason for Paul's Prayer (3:14-15)
- E. The Requests in Paul's Prayer (3:16-19)
    1. Inner Power from the Holy Spirit (3:16)
    2. Indwelling of Christ (3:17a)
    3. Knowledge of an Incomprehensible Love (3:17b-19a)
    4. God's Fullness (3:19b)
- F. The Conclusion of Paul's Prayer (3:20-21)

VII. Ephesians 4:1-16 – Living in Unity
- A. Walking in Unity (4:1-6)
- B. Walking in Maturity (4:7-16)

VIII. Ephesians 4:17-5:2 – Living in Purity
- A. Out With the Old; In With the New (4:17-24)
- B. Off With the Old; On With the New (4:25-5:2)
    1. Falsehood – Speaking Truth (4:25)

      2. Anger - Reconciliation (4:26-27)
      3. Stealing – Working Hard and Sharing (4:28)
      4. Unwholesome Talk – Encouraging Talk (4:29-30)
      5. Malice and Hatefulness – Kindness and Compassion (4:31-32)
      6. Imitate God (5:1-2)

IX. **Ephesians 5:3-21 – Living as Children of Light**
   A. Living as a Light of Purity (5:3-14)
      1. Avoid the Darkness of Sexual Immorality (5:3-7)
      2. Live in the Light of Righteousness (5:8-14)
   B. Living as a Light of Wisdom (5:15-21)
      1. Not Unwise, But Wise (5:15-16)
      2. Not Foolishly, But Understanding God's Will (5:17)
      3. Not Drunk with Wine, But Filled with the Spirit (5:18-21)

X. **Ephesians 5:21-6:9 – Living in Mutual Submission**
   A. Submitting to One Another (5:21)
   B. Submitting in Marriage (5:22-33)
      1. The Wife's Responsibility to Submit (5:22-24)
      2. The Husband's Responsibility to Submit (5:25-33)
   C. Submitting in the Family (6:1-4)
      1. The Child's Responsibility to Submit (6:1-3)
      2. The Parent's Responsibility to Submit (6:4)
   D. Submitting in the Workplace (6:5-9)
      1. The Servant's/Employee's Responsibility to Submit (6:5-8)
      2. The Master's/Employer's Responsibility to Submit (6:9)

XI. **Ephesians 6:10-20 – Living with Strength and Courage**
   A. Understanding the Battles We Face (6:10-13)
   B. Preparing for the Battles We Face (6:14-20)
      1. The Armor We Must "Put On" (6:14-15)

        a. The Belt of Truth (6:14a)
        b. The Breastplate of Righteousness (6:14b)
        c. The Shoes of Readiness (6:15)
    2. The Armor We Must "Take Up" (6:16-17)
        a. The Shield of Faith (6:16)
        b. The Helmet of Salvation (6:17a)
        c. The Sword of the Spirit (6:17b)
    3. The Prayers We Must "Always" Pray (6:18-20)

XII. Ephesians 6:21-24 – Closing Statements
    A. A Commendation of Tychicus (6:21-22)
    B. A Blessing of Peace, Love, and Grace (6:23-24)

Chapter I

Introduction to the Epistle to the Ephesians
Ephesians 1:1-2

A. *Background of the Letter to the Ephesians* (**Ephesians 1:1-2**)

1. AUTHORSHIP

   a. Verses 1-2 constitute the salutation of the letter and specifically identify the Apostle Paul as the author (1:1a).

      (1) Despite this clear statement of authorship, many scholars do not believe Paul actually wrote the letter, believing instead that it was written by one of Paul's disciples who used the apostle's name as a pseudonym.[1]

      (2) However, because Scripture explicitly identifies Paul as the author, the burden rests on those who dispute what the letter plainly declares to provide irrefutable proof otherwise. Each of the reasons typically given for disputing Paul's authorship of Ephesians can be rebutted, so there are no justifiable reasons to doubt Scripture's claim that Paul is the author of the letter.[2]

b. Paul described himself as "an apostle of Christ Jesus by the will of God" (1:1b).

(1) The Greek word translated "apostle" (*apostolos*) was originally used to describe a person who was sent as a representative or messenger of the one sending him or her.[3] Over time it came to refer specifically to a special messenger of Jesus Christ to whom Jesus delegated authority to perform special tasks on His behalf.

(a) This latter meaning corresponds to the Hebrew concept of a *shaliach*, a term that referred to someone who was given full authority to represent the person granting the authority. Jewish rabbis taught that a man's *shaliach* was the same as the man himself.[4]

(b) Thus, Paul claimed to be an authorized messenger for Christ—the *shaliach* of Jesus Christ—delivering the message of Christ as though Christ Himself was delivering it.

(2) Not only did Paul claim to be an apostle but he asserted that his apostleship was solely the result of "the will of God."[5] In other words, there was no personal merit on Paul's part that qualified him to claim this authority. He was commissioned by God as an apostle simply because God chose him.

2. WHEN AND WHERE WRITTEN. Paul likely wrote the letter while he was in prison (or, more specifically, under house arrest) in Rome around 61-62 A.D.[6]

3. RECIPIENTS

   a. Paul addressed the letter to believers whom he called "holy people" (1:1c) and "the faithful in Christ Jesus" (1:1d). (Some translations say "saints" (ESV, NASB) rather than "holy people.")

   (1) These terms were meant to be taken synonymously in order to refer to the readers as people who were set apart by God as opposed to having any special status of sainthood or character of moral perfection. In short, the recipients were believers and followers of Jesus Christ first, and because of their commitment to Christ they were declared holy by God.

   (a) The phrase "the faithful" referred primarily to people who placed their faith in Christ rather than to persons who were reliable and trustworthy.[7]

   (b) Pastor H.A. Ironside explains, "It is faith in Christ Jesus which constitutes a person a saint. ... We do not become saints by saintliness, but we should be characterized by saintliness because we are saints."[8]

   (2) The phrase "in Christ Jesus" is a significant one throughout the book of Ephesians. Paul used the phrase thirty-six times in the letter, more than in any other letter he wrote.[9] It is a term that describes our *position* in Christ rather than our *belief* in Him. Consequently,

   > **What does it mean to be "in Christ"?**

the phrase focuses primarily on the unity and identity believers have with Christ. Paul's emphasis throughout the book of Ephesians, as it is here in verse 1, was always about the believers' position of being united with Christ.[10]

b. Where these saints were located is a more difficult issue than it may appear because the words "in Ephesus" are not in the earliest manuscripts. The best explanation is that the letter was not written to a particular church. Instead, it was a circular letter that was sent and delivered to several different churches, one of which was Ephesus.[11]

(1) Since Tychicus was likely the one who carried the letter (see Ephesians 6:21) as he headed toward Colosse (see Colossians 4:7), it is believed he took this letter to the churches he visited

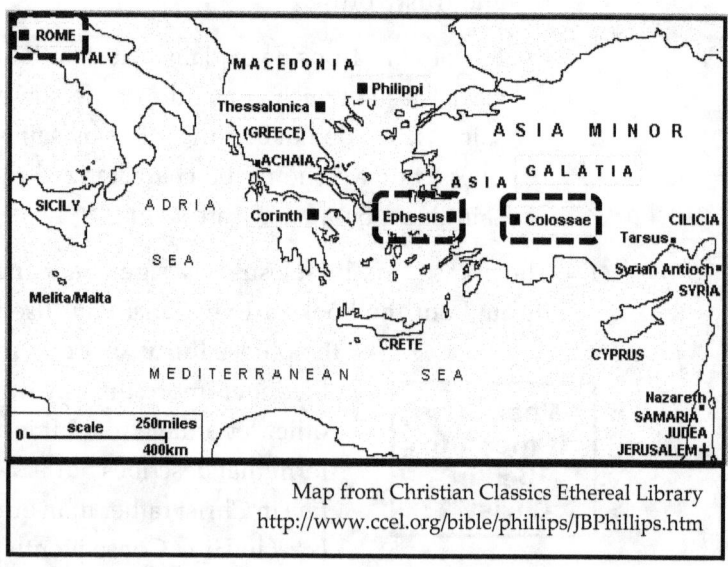

Map from Christian Classics Ethereal Library
http://www.ccel.org/bible/phillips/JBPhillips.htm

along the route from Rome to Colosse in southwest Asia Minor, including Ephesus.[12] According to this view, the location was left blank in the original letter, and Tychicus filled in the church name when he stopped to read and deliver the letter at each location.[13] The Ephesus copy, in such a case, was the only one that survived.

(2) A different explanation for the letter's destination is this letter is the one referred to in Colossians 4:16 that was intended for Laodicea but ultimately made its way to Ephesus.

c. Regardless of the letter's original destination, it is appropriate that it is identified with Ephesus because the city of Ephesus was the largest and most prominent city in the region. Approximately three hundred thousand people lived there, and it housed the highly influential Temple of Diana (or Artemis), one of the Seven Wonders of the Ancient World. The city was a major center for banking, commerce, government, and religion in the Roman world and became a major base of operations for Paul and later Christians as they evangelized Asia Minor.[14]

4. GREETING. Paul greeted the Ephesians with his standard greeting, wishing them "grace and peace ... from God our Father and the Lord Jesus Christ" (1:2).[15]

   a. Grace is the receipt of something we do not deserve.

   b. Peace is an inner stillness that is not affected by outward circumstances.

B. *Purpose of the Book of Ephesians*

1. Of all Paul's letters, Ephesians was the most general in nature. Paul did not address any particular problem among the readers or the churches in the letter. However, because he wrote the letter to the Ephesians around the same time he wrote his epistle to the Colossians, it is possible Paul's primary purpose for writing the Ephesians letter was similar to his purpose for writing to the Colossians.

    a. Paul wrote the Colossian believers to encourage them not to be led astray by any "hollow and deceptive philosophy" (Colossians 2:8) and to "continue to live in [Christ], rooted and built up in him, strengthened in the faith you were taught, and overflowing with thankfulness" (Colossians 2:6-7).

    b. If he had the same or a similar purpose for the letter to the Ephesians, then Paul's intent was to encourage his readers to recognize the blessings they received "in Christ" and to live in accordance with them.[16]

2. Consequently, the purpose or message of Ephesians has been expressed in various ways:

    a. To describe the believers' reconciliation with Christ and their unity in Him.[17]

    b. To encourage Gentile Christians by explaining that they have a place in God's eternal plan and, as a result, they also have a responsibility to live in accordance with their position in God's plan.[18]

    c. To do what commentator Klyne Snodgrass called "identity formation" by reminding believers of who they are in terms of their relationship with Christ and of their responsibility to conform their lifestyle into one that is consistent with their identity in Him.[19]

C. *General Outline of the Book of Ephesians.* The Book of Ephesians is easily divided into two parts. Chapters 1-3 constitute the doctrinal part of the letter, focusing on the believer's riches and position in Christ. Chapters 4-6 concentrate on practical application, describing how a believer should use those riches and position in his or her everyday life.

A Quick Glance at Ephesians

WHO was the author?	WHO were the recipients?
The Apostle Paul (1:1)	"The saints in Ephesus" (1:1)
	Probably a "circular letter"
	Ephesus: largest and most prominent city in western Asia minor; a major banking and religious center
WHEN was the letter written?	**WHY was the letter written?**
During Paul's first imprisonment in Rome, around A.D. 61	No particular problem or controversy addressed
	To encourage the readers to recognize the blessings they have "in Christ" and to instruct them on how to live in accordance with those blessings
WHAT is the basic outline of the letter?	**WHAT is the major theme of the letter?**
The Blessings of God's People (chs. 1-3)	The Church: the Body of Christ
The Conduct of God's People (chs. 4-6)	

A One-Sentence Summary of the Letter

Ephesians describes the spiritual blessings believers have received and their responsibilities of being a part of the Body of Christ.

Ephesians 1:1-2

Questions for Personal Reflection or Group Discussion

1. *Eph. 1:1a:* What is the significance of Paul identifying himself as "an apostle of Christ Jesus"?
2. *Eph. 1:1b:* Paul said he was an apostle "by the will of God"? How does it change your perspective if you saw yourself as being called to your career and profession "by the will of God"?
3. *Eph. 1:1c:* How can you apply in your own life H.A. Ironside's statement about believers being saints: "We do not become saints by saintliness, but we should be characterized by saintliness because we are saints"?
4. *Eph. 1:1d:* What does it mean to be "in Christ"? As a believer, how does the term describe your relationship with God?

Chapter II

Every Spiritual Blessing in Christ
Ephesians 1:3-14

A. *Praise to God* **(Ephesians 1:3)**. After his salutation, Paul launched into a lengthy tribute of praise to God.[1]

1. PRAISE EXPRESSED. The New International Version translates the opening words of verse 3 as "praise be." In the original Greek, the word actually used is "bless" (*eulogetos*), which literally means "to speak well of." Paul used it three times in verse 3: "*Blessed* be the God and Father of our Lord Jesus Christ, who has *blessed* us in Christ with every spiritual *blessing* in the heavenly places" (ESV, emphasis added).

2. PRAISE TO WHOM? Paul praised "the God and Father of our Lord Jesus Christ," whom he further described as the One "who has blessed us." Paul elaborated on the specific blessings received from God in the subsequent verses. The source of these blessings is God the Father, who is worthy of our praise and adoration because, among other reasons, He has given us the incredible blessings.

   a. The blessings God has given us are described in verse 3 in general terms as "every spiritual blessing in Christ." The word "every" is the Greek word *pa-*

se, which means "all, every, the whole." It is an all-inclusive term.

(1) Each of these spiritual blessings is the result of God's saving act through Jesus Christ, and every believer has received all of them.

(2) The significance of this truth is overwhelming. It means we already possess many of the things we continually ask God for. In other words, when we ask God for peace or joy or strength, we are asking for blessings God has already given us. We cannot receive more of them; we simply have to learn how to implement what we already possess.

(3) The description of them as "spiritual blessings" was not intended as a contrast from material blessings or as a reference to spiritual gifts only. Instead it was a description of the source of the blessings—the Holy Spirit, whom Paul described in fuller detail later in the passage.[2]

b. The blessings were given "in the heavenly realms," a phrase that has important connotations. These blessings are not promised to us only when we get to heaven, but are available to us today and now. Thus, the phrase is metaphorical in a sense, linking the blessings of our salvation today with the heavenly benefits we will enjoy in the eternal future.[3] It means our blessings are a spiritual reality for us now and, as a result, we are able to enjoy the benefits of heaven to come even in this life today.[4]

> **In what ways are we able to enjoy the benefits of heaven today?**

c. The sole means by which these blessings come is through our connection "in Christ." There would be no blessings for us at all without Christ, His work of salvation on our behalf, and our resulting union in and with Him.[5] These are blessings, therefore, only for the saved, whom Paul called "God's holy people," or the "saints" (ESV, NASB, CSV), in Ephesians 1:1.

3. PRAISE WITH EXCITEMENT. Verses 3-14 constitute one long sentence in the original Greek—over 200 words.

   a. Theologians have various linguistic explanations for the extreme length of the sentence, but it appears it was the result of Paul's growing excitement as he began listing and describing each spiritual blessing God has given us. As he did so, one thought led to another thought, which led to another, and then to another, etc. Moreover, the long, run-on sentence evidences the way God's work and blessings are interwoven and interconnected.

   b. Beginning in verse 4, Paul listed the spiritual blessings God blessed us with. The passage in Ephesians 1:3-14 can be divided into three Trinitarian segments: the blessings of God the Father (1:3-6), of Jesus Christ (1:7-12), and of the Holy Spirit (1:13-14).

B. *The Blessings of God the Father* (Ephesians 1:4-6)

1. GOD CHOSE US (1:4)

   a. The idea of God choosing us is called the "doctrine of election." The concept is also mentioned in verses 5 and 11 by the word "predestined."

(1) At the beginning of the letter, Paul immediately plunged his readers into one of the most difficult concepts in the Bible. The doctrine of election and its relationship to the doctrine of free will is one of the more challenging teachings in Scripture to understand, along with concepts such as Jesus' simultaneous divinity and humanity, the Trinity, and similar issues. There are, however, certain aspects of the doctrine of election that are clear.

   (a) First, we should consider what the doctrine does not mean. Election and predestination do not refer to God's foreknowledge.

      i. We are not chosen because God already knew we would accept Him. This gives us too much credit for attaining our salvation.

      ii. Nor does the doctrine of election suggest God chose us because He knew we could help Him accomplish His will. God does not need us to accomplish anything for Him.

   (b) Essentially, the doctrine of election means exactly what it says: we were not saved by our own merits or actions but as a result of God's grace in choosing us. We cannot be saved unless God first chooses us. Jesus explained it this way: "No one can come to me unless the Father who sent me draws him" (John 6:44).

      i. Does this doctrine diminish our free will? No. Clearly, the Bible teaches that we must accept Jesus in order to be saved.[6] But, we do not have the option to accept Him unless God first chooses to give us that option.

ii. Election does not mean God chooses to save some people and not others or to give some the option to be saved while giving no such option to others. There is nowhere in Scripture in which the doctrine of election is mentioned in connection with a person's ability to find salvation.[7] In other words, a person is not elected and then saved. Instead, the person is saved first and, then, as a consequence, becomes the elect.[8]

(A) In fact, most references in the Bible to election deal with God's choosing a group of people. For example, God selected the Israelites to be His chosen people (Deuteronomy 7:6), and He chose New Testament believers by His grace (see Romans 11:5).

(B) Additionally, references to predestination usually refer to God's designs for believers, such as His plan to adopt us (see Ephesians 1:5) or to conform us to the likeness of Christ (see Romans 8:29). Thus, God elects people and predestines the gloriousness of their futures.

iii. In reality, there is no way we can reconcile in our limited human minds the biblical truths of God's sovereign election and man's free will. Attempts to do so by theologians and Bible teachers over the centuries generally result in lessening the importance of one or the other of the doctrines or watering down the meaning of both doctrines by seeking a compromise between them. The correct response we should have is to accept both truths completely, trust God to harmonize them, and praise Him for His superiority over our finite minds to reconcile what is seemingly irreconcilable.

iv. Our inability to understand how these two truths work together, however, is not a reason for us to become careless and unthinking in our faith. The Apostle Peter commanded us to "make every effort to confirm your calling and election" (2 Peter 1:10) by living faithful lives exhibited in goodness, knowledge of God's will, self-control, perseverance, godliness, and love (see 2 Peter 1:5-7). To do so requires us to study and seek to understand God's Word and His truths as best we can through the ministry of the Holy Spirit in our lives.

b. Paul mentioned three elements in verse 4 pertaining to God's choosing of believers:

(1) *How We Were Chosen.* We were chosen "in Him." These riches are given to us only because of what Jesus did and only if we are identified with Jesus and have submitted our lives to Him.

(2) *When We Were Chosen.* We were chosen "before the creation of the world." In other words, we are not an afterthought to God. He has known us and loved us from the beginning.

  (a) This fact emphasizes our total lack of merit or self-achievement regarding our salvation. To be chosen is entirely the result of God's grace and has nothing to do with anything we have done to earn or deserve salvation.

  (b) Being chosen by God also should help us see how special we are to God. God chose us before we had the chance to do anything in order to please Him. Thus, He chose us simply because He loves us as we are.[9]

  (c) Having been chosen "before the creation of the world" further suggests the completeness and permanence of our salvation. To a timeless God, once we are saved, not only will we continue to be saved forever, but in God's mind, we have been saved since "before the creation of the world."

> **What does the fact that God chose us "before the creation of the world" tell us about how God views us?**

(3) *Why We Were Chosen.* We were chosen for the purpose of being "holy and blameless in God's sight." We were not chosen simply to avoid hell

and get to heaven but in order to live changed lives. As a result of being chosen, we inherit the responsibility to live holy and blameless lives before God.

(a) "Holy" means we are set apart. It does not imply we are to be *separated from* the world, but that we are to be *different* from the world in terms of our character, attitudes, beliefs, and actions.

(b) "Blameless" does not mean we are sinless, but that "in God's sight" we are without blame for our sins. What an incredible gift! The Greek word for "blameless" (*anomous*) means "without blemish" and is reminiscent of the requirement in the Old Testament that animal sacrifices offered to God be unblemished.

  i. The result of Christ's work on our behalf is that we will be able to stand before God in the final day as "holy and blameless" individuals. In Colossians 1:22, Paul said, "He has reconciled you by Christ's physical body through death to present you holy in his sight, without blemish and free from accusation."

  ii. But Paul's focus in Ephesians 1:4 on what we have been chosen to become in the future does not remove the responsibility we have to live holy and blameless lives now. In Romans 12:1, Paul urged believers to "offer your bodies as a living sacrifice, holy and pleasing to God" (Romans 12:1). We cannot escape our responsibility to live in accordance with God's intentions for us today.[10]

    (c) "In his sight" refers to God's perfect moral judgment. Because He chose us, God sees us as being holy and blameless even though we are undeserving of such a gracious and merciful verdict. In essence, God sees us through a lens that is coated by Christ's perfect righteousness.

c. *The Significance of This Blessing:* What is the significance of God choosing us?

  (1) Being chosen reflects how valuable, special, and important we are to God. It should negate feelings of low self-esteem and low value.

  (2) Being chosen clearly reveals the fact that we have done nothing in and of ourselves to deserve the value God places upon us. Consequently, God's love and acceptance of us is granted to us without conditions.[11]

2. GOD ADOPTED US (1:5)

a. Paul said we have been "predestined" for adoption. Again, as mentioned earlier, this has nothing to do with a choice by God to adopt or save some people and not others. Instead, it refers to God's predetermination that all who are saved will be fully adopted into His family.

  (1) To be adopted means God has brought us into His family as full-fledged children with all the rights and benefits of natural-born children. Not

only have we been pardoned for our offenses against God, but we have been given a new identity as children of God.

(2) Our adoption is "through Jesus Christ," which means it is accomplished only because and by means of what Jesus did for us through His death and resurrection.

(3) We have been adopted "in accordance with his pleasure and will." These words are more than just a statement of volition on God's part. They suggest it was truly God's heart desire to bring us into His family. God finds great joy in blessing us.

b. *The Significance of This Blessing:* What is the significance of God adopting us?

(1) Our adoption by God evidences the strength and permanence of our relationship to God.

(2) It gives us a sense of belonging and stability and should offset any doubts and uncertainty we may have of who we are in life.

3. GOD GAVE US HIS GRACE (1:6)

a. God's grace is free, but it is available only "in the One he loves," i.e., Jesus.

b. What is grace? It is something given to us that we do not deserve. In this instance, God has given us our election and adoption. Clearly, we did not receive these things because we deserve them since they were made available to us before we were even born. Likewise, we cannot do anything to continue to receive or keep His grace. Otherwise, it no longer constitutes grace.

c. *The Significance of This Blessing:* What is the significance of God giving us grace? It highlights the fact that we do not have to do or be anything to receive God's love and mercy. This spiritual treasure should counteract any feelings of inadequacy we have and help us recognize the futility of trying to earn God's favor through our works.

C. *The Blessings of Jesus Christ* (**Ephesians 1:7-13a**)

1. CHRIST REDEEMED US (1:7-8)

   a. The redemption Paul spoke about in verse 7 was similar to the redemption available to slaves in his day.[12] A slave could be bought by a member of his family or some other benefactor and then set free. Thus, to be redeemed implied LIBERATION from slavery. In a spiritual sense, we were once slaves to sin and have been redeemed—liberated—from that slavery.[13]

   (1) Our redemption price was essentially a ransom paid by Jesus "through His blood."

   (a) In the Old Testament, a blood sacrifice was essential for paying the price for sins.[14] But the sacrifice had to be something that had intrinsic value to be worthy of paying the price. That is why the Old Testament animal sacrifices were inadequate for any long-lasting redemptive purpose, and why Jesus's sacrifice was infinitely sufficient.

   (b) Jesus died because we were condemned to die. As Paul explained in 2 Corinthians 5:21: "God made him who had no sin to be sin for us, so that in him we might become the righteousness of God."

(2) Having been redeemed, the price for our sins has been "paid in full." Thus, our debts to God have been FORGIVEN.

b. Redemption and forgiveness are given to us "in accordance with the riches of God's grace."

(1) He did not merely give *out of* His riches (i.e., He did not only share with us a portion of what He had), but He gave *according to* His riches (i.e., He gave in total agreement and conformity with the riches of His grace).

Ironside illustrates the distinction between these two terms this way: "Here is a millionaire to whom you go on behalf of some worthy cause. He listens to you and says, 'Well, I think I will do a little for you,' and he takes out his pocketbook and selects a ten-dollar bill. Perhaps you had hoped to receive a thousand from him. He has given you *out* of his riches, but not *according* to his riches. If he gave you a book of signed blank checks all numbered, and said, 'Take this, fill in what you need,' that would be *according* to his riches."[15]

(2) God "lavished" these riches on us. In other words, God's redemption, liberation, and forgiveness are showered on us in superabundance.

(3) God lavished these spiritual riches on us "with all wisdom and understanding."[16]

(a) "Wisdom" is the "ability to see life from God's perspective," while "understanding" refers more specifically to the "ability to discern the right action to take in any given situation."[17] It may be, however, the two words are not intended to convey different meanings but instead constitute a literary device called a hendiadys, by which a single idea is conveyed by two separate words (such as "a nice and warm day"). The single idea in this instance is God's gift of insight for how to live wisely and in accordance with His will.[18]

(b) In other words, God does not merely save us and then leave us to our own devices to figure out how to live afterwards. God provides everything we need to know Him and obey Him.

c. *The Significance of This Blessing:* What is the significance of being redeemed, liberated, and forgiven? The significance is immeasurable! We are saved for eternity with no liability or culpability for our sins. As a result, we are freed from guilt for our past and need have no fear about our future.

2. CHRIST INFORMED US OF GOD'S WILL (1:9-10)

a. Jesus Christ has revealed to us the "mystery of His will" (1:9), i.e., God's plan and purpose. The wisdom and understanding Christ provided with His grace helps us understand better God's purpose and will.

(1) A mystery, as used in the Bible, refers to a formerly hidden truth that has been revealed.[19]

The mystery Paul referred to in these verses was God's plan to bring everything in heaven and on earth into unity and under the headship of Jesus Christ (1:10).[20] In other words, nothing in this world has meaning apart from Christ, and nothing will provide life apart from Christ.

(2) This aspect of the mystery has not yet occurred, but God will accomplish His plan in His own timing. The Greek word translated in the New International Version as "to be put into effect" (*oikonomian*) (1:10) is often used with respect to the management of a household or estate. It conveys the meaning that God is in control and managing everything that is happening to ensure that His plan will be accomplished "when the times reach their fulfillment" (1:10), i.e., at a time still future that God will determine.

b. *The Significance of This Blessing:* How does being informed help us in our daily lives? It gives us peace and comfort in the midst of trials because we know God is in control and we understand—at least in a general way—what He is accomplishing. Consequently, having such knowledge helps allay our feelings of confusion and fear about life and all that happens to us.

3. CHRIST INCLUDED US IN THE GOSPEL (1:11-13a)

a. The pronouns used in verses 11-13 and the following verses suggest a distinction made by Paul between the Jews ("we") and the Gentiles ("you"). In other words, Paul referred to the fact that Israel ("we") was chosen by God to bring praise to His name, and the Gentiles ("you") were included in this election once they heard the gospel and believed it.[21]

b. Our inclusion, therefore, means, like the Jews originally, we have been APPOINTED by God to testify to the world about God's plan and purpose. We have a job to do, both by our lifestyle and our words.

c. *The Significance of This Blessing:* What is the significance of being included in God's plans and appointed by Him to spread His gospel message? Our inclusion and consequent appointment means we have a purpose of great and eternal significance. As a result, this blessing should nullify any feelings of unimportance and meaninglessness we may have in our lives.

\	Our Spiritual Blessings from God (1:3-14)		
God the Father	He Chose Us	He Adopted Us	He Gave Us Grace
God the Son	He Redeemed Us	He Informed Us	He Included Us
God the Holy Spirit	He Sealed Us	He Guaranteed Our Redemption	

D. *The Blessings of the Holy Spirit* (Ephesians 1:13b-14)

1. THE HOLY SPIRIT SEALED US (1:13b). Verse 13 does not actually say the Holy Spirit sealed us but that the Holy Spirit *is* the seal. We received the Holy Spirit when we believed the "message of truth" (1:13a).

   a. Seals in Paul's day had several purposes: to authenticate or certify documents, to identify ownership, to make something secure, and to convey authority. These functions mirror the purposes of the Holy Spirit's seal in believers' lives.

      (1) *Authentication.* Having the Holy Spirit in our lives authenticates (i.e., certifies) us as being true believers. The Apostle John said, "We know that we live in him and he in us, because he has given us of his Spirit" (1 John 4:13).

      (2) *Identification.* Having the Holy Spirit in our lives identifies us as belonging to God. As Paul told the Romans, "The Spirit himself testifies with our spirit that we are God's children" (Romans 8:16).

      (3) *Security.* Having the Holy Spirit in our lives secures us in our salvation. Just as ancient kings placed their seals on those places that were to be safeguarded against disturbance by outsiders (see, e.g., King Darius' seal placed on the stone covering the entrance to the lions' den in Daniel 6:17 or Pilate's seal placed on the stone safeguarding Christ's tomb in Matthew 27:65-66), God's seal of the Holy Spirit on our hearts "marks" us as belonging to Him and secures us in Christ from outside disturbances that would prevent us from attaining "our inheritance."[22]

(4) *Authority.* Having the Holy Spirit in our lives gives us the authority to speak and act on God's behalf and with His authority. Jesus described this authority in Act 1:8, where He said, "But you will receive power when the Holy Spirit comes on you; and you will be my witnesses in Jerusalem, and in all Judea and Samaria, and to the ends of the earth."

b. *The Significance of This Blessing:* What is the significance of being sealed by the Holy Spirit? Having been sealed, our salvation is certified and secured. Therefore, we can be certain of our salvation and need not have any doubts about God's acceptance of us.

2. THE HOLY SPIRIT GUARANTEED OUR REDEMPTION (1:14)

a. Paul described the Holy Spirit as a "deposit, guaranteeing our inheritance." Other translations use the word "pledge" (NASB) or "down payment" (ESV, CSB). A deposit was used, in Paul's day, as a down payment for making a contract, promising to fulfill an obligation, or sampling what was to come.[23]

> **The Holy Spirit is God's down payment of His promises to us in Heaven.**

(1) The Holy Spirit is God's down payment of His promises to us—His pledge to fulfill those promises—and a sample, or foretaste, of what is yet to come.[24] As Matthew Henry explains, "The earnest [or down payment or pledge] is part of payment, and it secures the full sum: so is the gift of the

Holy Ghost .... The Spirit's illumination is [a down payment] of everlasting light; sanctification is [a down payment] of perfect holiness; and his comforts are [down payments] of everlasting joys."[25]

(2) The Greek word used for "deposit" or "pledge" is *arrabon*, which is the same word used for an engagement to marriage. Within that context, the Holy Spirit's presence in our lives can be viewed as" an engagement ring" that symbolizes our promised future marriage with Jesus Christ.[26]

b. The Spirit-deposit is a guarantee that we will receive our full "inheritance" at the time of "the redemption of those who are God's possession." This was Paul's reference to the final step in salvation when we will be freed from the presence of sin.

c. *The Significance of This Blessing:* What is the significance of the Holy Spirit's guarantee? The fact that God would provide a down payment for His promises in order to assure us He will keep them sends us a strong message of how much God wants us to be free from worry and doubt about our salvation and future and how much He desires us to trust Him.

Questions for Personal Reflection or Group Discussion

1. *Eph. 1:3:* The idea that God has given us "every spiritual blessing in Christ" is mindboggling. What reactions do you have to that truth?
2. *Eph. 1:3:* In what ways are we able to enjoy the benefits of heaven today?
3. *Eph. 1:4:* What does the fact that God chose you "before the creation of the world" say about how God views you?
4. *Eph. 1:7:* What is the difference between God giving blessings *out of* His riches and *according to* His riches?
5. *Eph. 1:4-14:* Throughout this chapter, we have discussed the significance of each of the spiritual blessings. Perhaps you can think of other implications from the spiritual blessings outlined by Paul in this passage. How does being a recipient of these great spiritual blessings impact your life?
    a. Chosen
    b. Adopted
    c. Given grace
    d. Redeemed – Liberated – Forgiven
    e. Informed
    f. Included - Appointed
    g. Sealed
    h. Guaranteed

Chapter III

Paul's Prayer for Our Enlightenment
Ephesians 1:15-23

A. *The Reasons for Paul's Gratitude* (**Ephesians 1:15-16**). Following the lengthy sentence in the Greek from verse 3 through verse 14, Paul finally took a breath and began another long sentence. Verses 15-23 also constitute a single sentence in the original Greek and the continuation of his thoughts in verses 3-14. After describing the spiritual blessings given to us by God, Paul expressed gratitude for his readers and prayed for them to fully understand and appreciate those blessings. Paul based his gratitude on three things:

1. THE APPLICABILITY OF THE BLESSINGS LISTED IN VERSES 3-14 (1:15a). Paul started this passage with the words "for this reason" or "therefore." His expression of gratitude was based upon the fact that his readers had received the spiritual blessings described in verses 3-14. In other words, he was saying, "Since all believers have been chosen and adopted and redeemed and sealed, etc. ..., I thank God for your faith in God and love for one another."

2. THEIR FAITH IN THE LORD (1:15b). Paul was not simply told that the Ephesians had faith, but he also heard reports of actual evidence of the Ephesians' faith. The fact there was such evidence meant their faith was more than just a mere declaration of belief but was also an active faith producing results. This kind of faith was cause for Paul's thanksgiving to God.

3. THEIR LOVE FOR ALL THE SAINTS (1:15c-16). Paul expressed gratitude because their faith was also evidenced by their love for other believers. His prayer is a reminder that our love for other believers is one of the primary indications of our salvation as well.[1] As the Apostle John explained, "Everyone who loves has been born of God and knows God. Whoever does not love does not know God, because God is love" (1 John 4:7-8).

B. *The Content of Paul's Prayer* **(Ephesians 1:17-23).** Because of his gratitude for his readers' faith and love, Paul regularly prayed for them, praying they would fully comprehend and utilize the spiritual blessings they already possessed. He did not pray for them to receive new blessings, but instead for them to understand what God had already done for them. As Pastor John Stott puts it: "What Paul does in Eph. 1, and therefore encourages us to copy, is both to keep praising God that in Christ all spiritual blessings are ours and to keep praying that we may know the fullness of what he has given us."[2] In particular, Paul prayed for these believers to receive two things:

1. WISDOM AND REVELATION (1:17). Paul prayed God would give his readers "the Spirit of wisdom and revelation."

a. It is not clear whether the "spirit" reference in this verse is to the Holy Spirit (as in Isaiah 11:2) or to simply "a spirit" or attitude. It probably does not matter for purposes of understanding the meaning, although Paul seemed focused on the spiritual gifts God bestows upon us rather than traits within us. If that is the case, Paul's reference was to the wisdom and revelation imparted by the Holy Spirit.[3]

b. As in Ephesians 1:8, "wisdom" refers to a believer's ability to see life from God's perspective.[4] "Revelation" refers to the spiritual insight a believer has about God and His truth. Without revelation from the Holy Spirit, it is impossible to truly grasp God's truths. Paul referred to this fact in 1 Corinthians 2:14, where he said, "The person without the Spirit does not accept the things that come from the Spirit of God but considers them foolishness, and cannot understand them because they are discerned only through the Spirit."

c. Such "wisdom and revelation" are needed "so that you may know [God] better" (1:17b). Paul wanted his readers to grow in their knowledge of God, to get to know Him better, and to increasingly grasp the meaning and depth of the love, grace, and blessings God had given them.

> **What is the difference between *knowing about* God and *experiencing* God?**

(1) There are different degrees of knowing and trusting God. When we only *know about* God, we probably do not trust Him fully when we face trials. But when we *experience* God, our trust in Him grows. This is like the difference between knowing a hot stove can burn you and touching a hot stove. The experience gives us a greater knowledge and appreciation of what the hot stove can do.

(2) In other words, having a non-experiential understanding of God adversely affects our faith and obedience. But as we come to know Him more intimately through experiences that reveal His work in our lives, the more we will love, trust, and obey Him.[5]

2. ENLIGHTENMENT (1:18a). Paul also prayed for God to enlighten the "eyes of your heart."

   a. What are the "eyes of your heart"? And what does it mean that they be enlightened?

      (1) The heart is considered the seat of our emotions, will, and motivations. Eyes are the means of perception and expression. Thus, to have the eyes of our hearts enlightened conveys the idea of illuminating our perception of spiritual matters.[6]

      (2) The Greek word for "enlightened" (*pephotismenous*) is a verb in the perfect tense, i.e., a tense conveying a past action with continuous results. It suggests that enlightenment is not a one-time event but must occur on an ongoing

Ephesians 1:15-23

basis to help us continue to grow in our understanding of the blessings God has given us.

b. Paul wanted us to be enlightened about three things God has given us. These three things constitute additional spiritual blessings and riches we possess.

(1) *Hope* (1:18b). Paul wanted us to know "the hope to which he has called you." This is not hope of *our* calling, but the hope of *His* calling, which is more comprehensive in scope. In other words, Paul prayed for his readers to understand the hope God gave them as a result of His calling them to salvation.[7]

(a) Hope does not mean wishful thinking or pining. In Scripture, hope generally refers to the assurance of a future event. We need to be enlightened in order to know that everything God has promised His chosen (or "called") ones will come true. God is faithful. Essentially, Paul prayed for us to understand the greatness of God's overall plan spelled out in Ephesians 1:3-14.

(b) *The Significance of This Blessing:* What does this kind of hope do for us in our daily lives? It should calm our fears about the future, focus our hearts and minds on heaven, and increase our trust in God. The hope God has given us significantly changes our eternal future for the better, which should, in response, change the way we live in the present.

(2) *Riches* (1:18c). Paul also wanted us to know "the riches of his glorious inheritance in the saints."[8]

(a) The entire letter speaks of the riches we have as a result of what Christ did for us and the blessings God poured out on us. Our riches are an inheritance from God, as Paul explained in Ephesians 1:14. In other words, the blessings and riches we receive from God are part of His current assets.

(b) In verse 18, though, Paul had a different focus, speaking of *God's* inheritance, not ours. We—as believers and thus "his holy people"—are God's inheritance. In other words, God treasures us and will "inherit" us by taking us to be with Him in heaven forever.[9]

(c) *The Significance of This Blessing:* What is the significance of having these spiritual riches and being an inheritance to God? As God's inheritance, we can be assured of how precious we are to Him. That assurance should help us overcome doubts about self-worth and low self-esteem and motivate us to serve Him.

(3) *Power* (1:19-23). The third thing Paul prayed his readers would understand better was "the immeasurable greatness of his power toward us who believe according to the working of his great might" (1:19 ESV).

(a) This is an incredible statement. We share in God's "incomparably great power" as believers. That power is the same power that raised Jesus from the dead (1:20a), exalted Jesus to a place of supreme honor and authority at the right hand of God above all earthly and spiritual powers (1:20b-21), and appointed Him head over everything (1:22). As participants in that power, we have been given the power to overcome any trial, rise above our circumstances, and experience victory even in the midst of apparent defeat, as long as we do not hinder this power by our worldliness and sin.

(b) Christ's appointment as ruler of all creation is "for the church" (1:22), i.e., for the benefit of the Church who shares in His authority.[10]

   i. Paul identified the Church as the body of Christ in Ephesians 1:23. Elsewhere, Paul referred to Christ as the "head" of the Church (see Colossians 1:18) to illustrate Christ's authority over believers. Here, though, Paul emphasized Christ's fellowship and unity with believers (i.e., the Church) by referring to the Church as His body.

   ii. One of the most difficult phrases in Ephesians to translate and interpret is the last part of Ephesians 1:23, which the New International Version translates this way: "the fullness of him who fills everything in every way."

(A) The questions about this passage primarily center on who the antecedent of "him" is. Is it Christ or God? In other words, is the Church the fullness of Christ, or is Christ the fullness of God?

(B) The term "fullness" generally refers to completeness or totality and is typically used throughout Scripture to refer to God's presence, essence, and glory.[11] Consequently, verse 23 probably refers to Christ as the fullness of God who fills everything with His presence. On the other hand, it also makes sense to understand the verse to mean that the Church is the fullness of Christ.[12] If the latter interpretation is the correct meaning of Paul's words, it suggests that the Church serves as the continuation of the incarnate Christ, responsible for doing what Christ would do by being His hands and feet (i.e., His body) in the world and serving as the full ex-

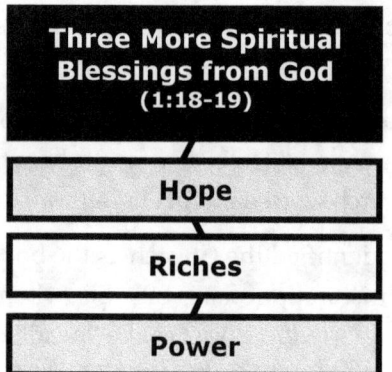

pression of Christ to a spiritually blind world.[13]

(c) *The Significance of This Blessing:* How does being a recipient of God's power impact our lives? Being recipients and participants in God's power should offset our feelings of insecurity and powerlessness. We possess the mightiest power and have access to the highest authority in the entire universe, so we are able to overcome any problems or trials that come our way. One commentator explains that having God's power means:

i. God is always ready to help us overcome every obstacle we face.

ii. God's power never stops and is always working for us.

iii. God is always fighting for us against the evil forces that oppose us.

iv. Nothing can stop or hinder God's power from accomplishing His will.[14]

Questions for Personal Reflection or Group Discussion

1. *Eph. 1:15:* What specific action did Paul identify as evidence of his readers' faith in Christ? How do you display this evidence of faith in your own life?
2. *Eph. 1:17:* Paul prayed for the Ephesians to receive "the Spirit of wisdom and revelation." What is "the Spirit of wisdom and revelation," and why does Paul want believers to obtain such wisdom and revelation?
3. *Eph. 1:18:* Paul prayed for "the eyes of your heart" to be enlightened. What does he want us to be enlightened about?
4. *Eph. 1:18-19:* As in the previous chapter, we addressed the significance of the various spiritual blessings God has given us. In this passage, Paul mentioned three additional spiritual blessings we have received. What does each of these blessings mean, and how does being a recipient of these spiritual blessings impact your life?
    a. Hope
    b. Riches
    c. Power

Chapter IV

From Death to Life
Ephesians 2:1-10

A. *What We Once Were* **(Ephesians 2:1-3).** In chapter 1, Paul described the believer's *possessions in Christ*. In chapter 2, he switched his emphasis to a believer's *position in Christ*.[1] To describe that position, Paul first explained to his readers their spiritual conditions prior to salvation (which serves as a description of anyone who is unsaved).

  1. DEAD (2:1). Paul described the basic human condition prior to salvation as being "dead in [our] transgressions and sins" (2:1).

    a. Paul's analysis of the human spiritual condition is simple and straightforward. According to Paul, humankind's problem is not that we are misguided, misled, confused, uneducated, or deprived of the resources we need in order to know God. Our problem simply is that, without God, we are dead.[2]

    b. Of course, Paul spoke on a spiritual level, talking of spiritual death that is characterized as a state of alienation and separation from God, or what Snodgrass calls a "meaningless life hardly worth living."[3]

c. The condition of death is caused by our "transgressions and sins" (2:1). These two terms constitute another hendiadys, a figure of speech used for emphasis by expressing a single idea with two words (e.g., "nice and warm"). Paul used the phrase, not only to highlight the individual sins we commit, but the overall concept of sinfulness and evil within all of humankind.[4]

d. Paul said we were dead *in* our transgressions and sins. We were not dead because *we committed* transgressions and sins; we were dead *in them*, which means that transgressions and sins were the result of an already existing sinful condition. In other words, human nature is sinful to begin with. We are not sinners because we sin; we sin because we are sinners.[5]

2. ENSLAVED TO EVIL (2:2-3a). We exhibited our "deadness" by enslavement to certain evil actions. Paul outlined three such actions that describe the characteristics of a life without Christ.

　a. We *"followed the ways of this world"* (2:2a). As sinners, we are conformists to the world around us. In his letter to the Romans, Paul said, "Do not conform to the pattern of this world, but be transformed by the renewing of your mind" (Romans 12:2a).

　b. *We followed Satan*, the "ruler of the kingdom of the air, the spirit who is now at work in those who are disobedient" (2:2b).

　　(1) The phrase "ruler of the kingdom of the air" is perhaps better translated "the prince [or ruler]

of the power [or authority] of the air" (see ESB, NASB). The ancient world believed the "air" was the space between heaven and earth—more particularly between the moon and earth—that served as the realm of the evil spirits.[6] The "ruler" was the one who controlled this evil domain, namely Satan. Some believe this is pictured in Job 1-2 when Satan appeared before God "from roaming through the earth" (Job 1:7).

(2) Paul spoke further about the rule of Satan over the world later in the letter, when he said, "For our struggle is not against flesh and blood, but against the rulers, against the authorities, against the powers of this dark world and against the spiritual forces of evil in the heavenly realms" (Ephesians 6:12).

c. *We followed our own sinful desires and thoughts,* "gratifying the cravings of our sinful nature [or flesh]" (2:3a). Not only were we led into disobedience by demonic powers, but we were also led astray by our basic nature of sinfulness. According to commentator William Barclay, "The flesh is anything in us which gives sin its chance; it is human nature without God. To live according to the dictates of the flesh is simply to live in such a way that our lower nature, the worst part of us, dominates our lives."[7]

3. OBJECTS OF GOD'S WRATH (2:3b). As dead people who were powerless and corrupt, the only options we had were to follow the world and Satan because we knew

no better. As a result, we were objects of God's wrath (2:3b).

    a. God's wrath is not merely the idea of being "zapped" by God as though God is an angry disciplinarian acting out of uncontrollable anger. That is not the way God works.

> **What is the wrath of God?**

       (1) God's wrath is the natural response that occurs when holiness is confronted with sin and evil.[8]

       (2) Some commentators describe God's wrath as the "law of consequences." In other words, God has put in place certain natural consequences that automatically happen when we sin. Such a description does not imply that God's wrath is an impersonal process or does not involve the personality and holiness of God. As sinners, we are punished by being made to undergo the consequences of our actions. For instance, Paul said in Romans 1:24, "God gave [man] over in the sinful desires of their hearts."

    b. Paul's description of humankind is certainly a bleak one. Humans are, in essence, a form of "walking dead" because humankind has chosen to push God aside and ignore Him in their world and lives. As a result, sinful humanity falls under God's wrath. But the good news of the rest of chapter 2 of Ephesians is that God refuses to stay pushed aside or ignored. Instead, He offers an alternative and a solution to humankind's dire situation.

B. *What We Have Become* (**Ephesians 2:4-10**). Having described what we once were, Paul then described what we have become because of God's mercy and love.⁹ There are probably no two words in Scripture that should excite us more and give us reason to breathe a huge sigh of relief than the words "But God."¹⁰ In contrast to God's wrath in verse 3, Paul began to speak of God's mercy and what His mercy does for us "because of his great love for us" (2:4).

1. BROUGHT TO LIFE ... (2:4-6). Being dead, God "made us alive with Christ" and He "raised us up with Christ and seated us with him in the heavenly realms" (2:5-6). These acts constitute elements of another spiritual blessing and asset that we have: LIFE.

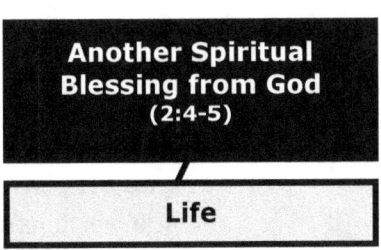

    a. We were made alive even when we were still dead in our transgressions and sins (2:5), which emphasizes the fact that our salvation is purely the result of God's grace. It also implies we do not have to be controlled by our sinful nature because we have the power to live in obedience to Christ rather than to the world or Satan or our sinful desires.

    b. We have been "raised up" to a new life, as new creatures (2:6a). We have been made alive in order to live in this world with new power. God did not simply take the sin problem away from us; He gave us the power to overcome it.

c. Further, we are seated with Christ (2:6b). Our spiritual resurrection is just as real and as complete as the physical resurrection and ascension of Christ.

2. ... FOR A PURPOSE (2:7-10). Why did God make us alive?

   a. God made us alive because He loves us (2:4). His actions on our behalf came "even when we were dead in transgressions" (2:5b). In other words, we were not seeking salvation when He first offered it to us. What a wonderful example of the unconditional nature of God's love and mercy.

   b. He made us alive in order to display to the rest of the world the "incomparable riches of His grace" (2:7). That display is necessary because, as Paul mentioned several times throughout these verses, all of this happens to us only by God's grace (2:8), not by any actions of our own. Consequently, there is no basis by which we can take credit for our salvation or boast about any of our achievements (2:9).

      (1) The *method* of our salvation is God's grace. We cannot be saved by any other method than to receive the undeserved gift of God's salvation, a gift He offers us solely because of His grace.

      (2) The *means* by which we access salvation is through faith.

         (a) Faith is more than mere assent or belief in certain ideas. The type of faith Paul spoke of involves trusting in one who is believed to be trustworthy. It means we bind ourselves to God and live in response to Him. This is part of the meaning Paul intended when he used the phrase "in Christ" throughout the letter.

(b) For believers who are familiar with verses 8-9, it can be easy to lose sight of how significant they are. Our familiarity with these verses tends to diminish their meaning and causes us to minimize the true meaning and significance of authentic, biblical faith. True faith is a faith centered on Jesus Christ, which is only then exemplified by an obedient lifestyle to God's expectations and demands of us.

(c) The object of our faith must be Jesus Christ. Faith by itself is insufficient to attain salvation unless our faith is centered on the Savior who has done the work to purchase our salvation.

c. He also made us alive so we would display His grace through our good works (2:10).

(1) In Ephesians 2:10, Paul said we are God's "handiwork" or, as other translations put it, "workmanship" (ESV, NASB). The Greek word is *poiema*, from which we get our English word "poem." In other words, we are God's poetry— His work of art—and we are on display to the world so the world will glorify the poet and artist: God.

> As believers, we are God's "poetry," His "work of art" on display to the world.

(2) Verse 10 points out that we are called to do good works. Such works are not in order *to receive* God's salvation, but the result of *having received* God's salvation.

(3) The closing statement in Ephesians 2:10, which says that these works have been "prepared [by God] in advance for us to do," does not mean God predetermines and predestines us to do the things we do. Yet its full meaning is difficult to understand, as demonstrated by the different translations of the text. The ESV and NASB say, "… which God prepared beforehand, that we should walk in them."

    (a) Some interpret verse 10 as meaning God prearranged for Christians to be "refashioned" in such a way that they are able to do good works that please God.[11]

    (b) More likely, however, its meaning is similar to the concept in Ephesians 1:4 of being chosen before the creation of the world. The verse suggests God prepared good works such as were necessary to accomplish His will, and when believers are made alive, they are then empowered to accomplish those works. Consequently, even the good deeds we perform cannot be attributed to our own determination, but solely to the grace of God.

(4) As we consider the important meaning of Ephesians 2:10, it should prompt us to pray each day a prayer of gratitude to God for the good works

He has prepared for us. In addition, we should ask Him to make us aware of what those good works are and grant us the strength and faithfulness to do them.

Questions for Personal Reflection or Group Discussion

1. *Eph. 2:1:* What is the human condition before receiving salvation in Christ? What does this mean?

2. *Eph. 2:2-3:* In what ways do those without Christ evidence their enslavement to evil?

3. *Eph. 2:2:* What does it mean to be a conformist to the world?

4. *Eph. 2:3:* How do you describe the wrath of God?

5. *Eph. 2:4-7:* An additional spiritual blessing God has given us is spiritual life. How does being a recipient of this blessing impact you?

6. *Eph. 2:4-7:* Why did God give us the blessing of spiritual life?

7. *Eph. 2:8-10:* What role do good works play in our salvation?

Chapter V

Jesus's Peace Mission
Ephesians 2:11-22

A. *Our Need for Reconciliation* (Ephesians 2:11-12)

1. History is replete with stories showing the hatred some people have for others and the urgent need for reconciliation between people. The infamous story of the West Virginia feud between the Hatfields and McCoys is such a story. The feud between these two families lasted almost thirty years and resulted in thirteen people killed, nine jailed, and one executed—all apparently triggered by the stealing of a pig![1]

2. Perhaps not quite as intensely violent as the Hatfield-McCoy feud, the resentment of the Jews toward the Gentiles was nonetheless just as impassioned. The Jews considered Gentiles no better than animals, and Gentiles despised the Jews for their religious snobbery.

    a. In Ephesians 1:10, Paul explained that God's ultimate plan is "to bring unity to all things in heaven and on earth under Christ." In order to create this reconciliation and unity, God must first subject the powers in heaven to Him ("things in heaven") and then establish one body among His believers ("things on earth").[2]

b. Beginning in Ephesians 2:11, Paul addressed the need for establishing reconciliation and unity among believers by returning to his description of the Gentiles' condition before they became Christians, focusing first on the animosity the Jews (who proudly called themselves the "circumcised" (2:11 CSB)) had for the Gentiles (whom the Jews derisively called the "uncircumcised" (2:11 CSB)). Paul minimized the importance of a distinction based upon circumcision by pointing out that such a distinction is man-made only. Instead, he urged the Gentiles to "remember" (2:12) where they came from rather than be sidetracked by the bitterness they felt over their mistreatment from the Jews.[3] Then Paul specifically described the Gentiles' situation prior to their salvation, which is another description (see Eph. 2:1-3) of all believers' conditions prior to being saved.

(1) *They were without Christ.* Paul said they were "separate from Christ" (2:12). Paul explained in Romans 1:18-23 that the Gentiles knew God but rejected Him. History is not a record of man starting with many gods and finding the true God. Instead, it is a history of being united with God (as Adam was in the Garden) and then rejecting Him (as Adam did in the Garden).

(2) *They were without citizenship.* Israel was God's chosen people. As unsaved Gentiles, they were without Christ, which meant they were "excluded from citizenship" (2:12) in God's Kingdom.

(3) *They were without a promise.* Not having citizenship with God's chosen people, they were "foreigners to the covenants of the promise" (2:12), which meant they had no access to the promises of God.

(4) *They were "without hope."* Since they were not recipients of God's promises of salvation, they were hopelessly left in their sins with no way out (2:12).

(5) *They were "without God."* Those who are unsaved typically have many different gods, but they do not have a relationship with the one and only true God (2:12).

B. *Christ's Work of Reconciliation* **(Ephesians 2:13-18).** As in Ephesians 2:4, Paul again used those two important words in verse 13: "But Christ." We who were "far away have been brought near" to God because of what Christ did for us.[4] The remaining verses in this passage describe Jesus' actions as something similar to a peace mission. In fact, an additional spiritual blessing God has given us is PEACE.

1. What is peace?

   a. The standard definition of peace is the absence of conflict and the existence of mutual harmony and agreement between people or nations.[5] But does the absence of conflict really constitute true peace?

   b. In Ephesians 2:14-16, Paul defined peace differently. He described God's peace as oneness. According to Paul, God "made the two groups one" (2:14) and created "in himself one new man out of the two, thus making peace" (2:15).

(1) This is dramatically different from the world's concept of peace. The world suggests peace occurs when adversaries refrain from fighting. God's peace, on the other hand, transforms warring factions into people who are united in purpose and in identity. UNITY is another spiritual blessing God has given us.

> **Peace is more than just the absence of conflict. God's peace results in unity between those who were once adversaries.**

(2) Consequently, Jesus accomplished a true peace between us and God. How significant is that? Not only does it mean we can go to heaven, but we can have peace of mind in this life because we know God is working for us, not against us.

2. The peace Paul talked about in this passage refers to the uniting of Gentiles and Jews into one body: the Church. But the work Jesus did also created a peace between man and God, and verses 13-18 speak of that as well.

3. How did Jesus accomplish this peace? He did it in three steps:

    a. First, He *broke down the walls* that separate us from God by destroying the "dividing wall of hostility" (2:14) created by the law and replacing those walls with grace and forgiveness (2:14-15a).[6]

(1) When speaking about the setting aside of the law (2:15), Paul likely referred, not to the abolition of the moral standards set by the Old Testament laws, but the abolition of the ritual requirements of the law that define whether a person was clean and saved.[7] We, too, are no longer subject to the Old Testament requirements for salvation.

(2) This also describes why peace is so often unattainable between nations, races, individuals, and spouses. Wars arise because of conflicting demands and requirements between parties who are acting from self-centered and self-righteous positions.[8] Peace comes when we abolish those requirements and selfish demands.

b. Second, He created a *"new humanity"* by uniting the two warring factions (2:15b) into a single body in Christ—a clear reference to the Church as the body of Christ. Here again is the reference to the creation of common purposes and goals, which creates harmony and unity.

c. Third, He *reconciled* us to God.

(1) Reconciliation means a restoration "to friendship or harmony."[9] It also refers to the balancing of accounts. In other words, Christ's work on our behalf balanced our spiritual account with God's. That means, amazingly, our sin list equals God's sin list: zero—not because we are without sin, but solely because Jesus paid for our sins.

(2) Jesus accomplished this "through the cross" (2:16). Consequently, RECONCILIATION is another spiritual blessing God has given us.

4. Peace is available, whether a person is Gentile ("far away") or Jew ("near"), only through Jesus, who provides us access to God (2:17-18).

    a. The Greek word for "access" is *prosagogen*, which referred to the right to freely approach a king. In the Persian royal court, an official called a prosagogeus led people into the king's presence to introduce them to him.[10] The Holy Spirit, therefore, serves as our prosagogeus, who introduces and presents us to God the Father.[11]

    b. ACCESS TO GOD is yet another spiritual blessing we have from God.

C. *The Results of Reconciliation* **(Ephesians 2:19-22).** What is the result of our reconciliation and peace? Paul used three metaphors to describe what it means to be at peace and reconciled with God and others:

1. We have become *citizens of God's kingdom* (2:19a). We are no longer foreigners. We have full rights of citizenship in God's Kingdom with God's people.

2. We have become *members of God's household* (2:19b). This is the adoption Paul mentioned in Ephesians 1:5.

3. We have become *building blocks in God's holy temple* (2:20-22).

    a. That means we are indwelt by God (2:22).

b. Likewise, the Church has become the dwelling place of God, and Jesus is the cornerstone of it (2:20-21).[12] In ancient times, the cornerstone was the first stone set in the foundation of a new building, serving as an important support for the building. It also became the reference point for setting all other stones in the foundation, thus determining the position of the entire structure.

c. Ironside addresses the impact of this truth by asking us to think about how we should respond to it. He says, "When you think of being a living stone in that glorious building, does it not bring to your soul a sense of the importance of holy living, of devotedness to Christ, of so behaving yourself that He will delight in dwelling in you?"[13]

D. *Lessons Learned from Being Reconciled*

1. THE RESPONSIBILITY OF BEING RECONCILED TO GOD. As members of the new body of Christ—the Church—we should take warning from the failures of Israel. The Jews were chosen by God to be a nation who would reveal God to the world by living lifestyles that were vastly different from those of the world.[14] Now, Gentiles have been united with believing Jews in the Church and share the same purpose: to reveal God to the world through our "different-ness" from the world. Does your life look different from the world?

2. THE RESPONSIBILITY OF BEING RECONCILED TO OTHER BELIEVERS. Part of the problem the Jewish and Gentile Christians had in Paul's day was the continuation of the racial barriers that divided them prior to their salvation. Paul explained, however, that Jesus did away with "Jew

and Gentile" and created something new and united. Today, we must be sure we do not build up walls and barriers to divide us from other believers, whether on the basis of denomination, race, gender, or culture. Those distinctions may cause us to worship differently, but they should never be used to divide us into warring camps.

3. THE RESULT OF BEING RECONCILED. Paul's explanation of the reconciliatory work of Christ is intended to incentivize us to become what we already are in Christ and then live accordingly, not only individually, but also in the community of all believers. Paul described what that means in more detail later in his letter.

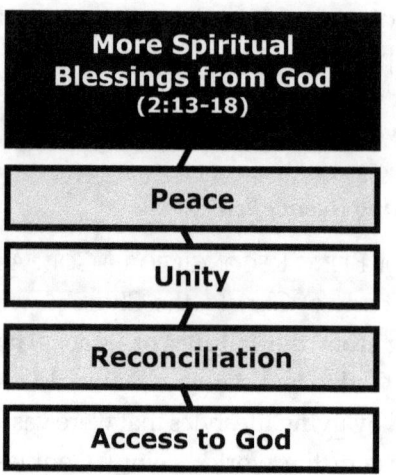

Questions for Personal Reflection or Group Discussion

1. *Eph. 2:12:* How did Paul describe the condition of those who are not saved?
2. *Eph. 2:14-16:* How did Paul define "peace"? How does his definition differ from the definition the world has for "peace"?
3. *Eph. 2:14-16:* What is the impact of the spiritual blessing of peace in your life?
4. *Eph. 2:14-16:* How did Jesus accomplish peace between us and God and between Jew and Gentile?
5. *Eph. 2:19-22:* What illustrations did Paul use to describe our peace and reconciliation with God and with others?
6. What are your thoughts about the lessons learned from being reconciled that are identified by the author? What other lessons and applications do you see from the truth of our reconciliation with God and with other believers?

Chapter VI

Paul's Prayer for Power
Ephesians 3:1-21

A. *Paul, the Prisoner of Christ* **(Ephesians 3:1).** Because of the reconciliation Jesus accomplished between Gentiles and Jews and between Gentiles and God ("For this reason"), Paul prayed a new prayer. Before he began his prayer, though, he identified himself as a "prisoner of Christ Jesus for the sake of you Gentiles."

1. Paul was in prison when he wrote the book of Ephesians, and he attributed his imprisonment to the Jews' opposition to his ministry to the Gentiles.[1]

    a. Thus, he identified himself as a "prisoner of Christ Jesus" rather than a prisoner of the Romans.

    (1) To Paul, Roman involvement in his imprisonment was merely incidental. Because Paul was bound to obey Christ's will, he viewed himself as Christ's prisoner because it was Christ's purpose for him to be in prison at the time. In fact, if not for him being in prison, he might never have written the letters of Ephesians, Philippians, Colossians, or Philemon.

(2) Paul's perspective of his actual imprisonment provides a wonderful example of how we, too, should view the trials we face in life.

(a) Perspective plays an important part in how we view life. An example is the story of an encounter Sir Christopher Wren—the famous architect who was hired to oversee the rebuilding of St. Paul's Cathedral in London—had with some of the workers on the Cathedral. One day when he was inspecting the work, he noticed that the quality of the work performed by three different brick layers was very different. He asked the first man what he was doing. "I am laying bricks," the man answered. When he asked the same question to the second bricklayer, who was doing a better job, he proudly replied, "I am working to feed my family." The third bricklayer was doing an almost perfect job. His reply exhibited a loftier perspective and purpose: "Sir, I am building a cathedral."²

(b) William Barclay says, "If a man is in prison for some great cause he may either grumblingly regard himself as an ill-used creature, or he may radiantly regard himself as the standard-bearer of some great cause. ... When we are undergoing hardship, unpopularity, material loss for the sake

> **What does Paul's description of himself as a "prisoner of Christ" teach us about the perspective we should have when we are going through trials?**

of Christian principles, we may either regard ourselves as the victims of men or as the champions of Christ."[3]

   b. The specific reason Paul said he was in prison was "for the sake of [the] Gentiles" since it was his preaching to the Gentiles that got him in trouble. He used his imprisonment to convey an authority he might not otherwise have. In other words, the fact Paul was imprisoned because of his love and service for the Gentiles served to affirm and strengthen what he had to say.[4]

2. Paul got sidetracked from his prayer, though, and provided a brief aside about the availability of the gospel to the Gentiles and how he came to learn of its availability. Paul did not return to his prayer until verse 14.

B. *Paul, the Steward of God's Mystery* **(Ephesians 3:2-7).** At the beginning of his digression, Paul described how God revealed to him "the mystery of Christ" (3:4). Earlier I defined a mystery as a formerly hidden truth that has been revealed. In Ephesians 1:9-10, Paul referred to the mystery as God's plan to bring everything in heaven and on earth under the headship of Jesus Christ. In these verses, the mystery is described as the availability of the riches of the gospel to the Gentiles (3:6). This is not a different mystery but the same mystery explained from a different perspective.

   1. Paul explained that God gave him a responsibility with respect to this mystery, which he defined as "the administration of God's grace" (3:2). Other versions translate "administration" as the "stewardship of God's grace" (ESV, NASB).

       a. Consequently, Paul felt a specific responsibility, not only to proclaim the mystery, but also to take care of it in such a way that it was clearly communicated and received by those who needed to hear it (3:7).

       b. Paul's example is a good one for the Church and Christians today. Being recipients of God's grace means we, too, are administrators, stewards, and managers of it as well. Grace is not only a tremendous gift we received, but it comes with a corresponding responsibility to actively use that grace in order to accomplish the work God has called us to do.

  2. Paul explained that the mystery of the inclusion of the Gentiles into the promises of God was revealed to the apostles and to the prophets (3:3-5).[5] While Paul's reference to "prophets" likely referred to the New Testament variety, the Old Testament prophets also had some idea of the availability of the gospel to Gentiles, which raises the question of how Paul considered the mystery to be recently revealed? While the Old Testament prophets understood God had a plan to bring salvation to the Gentiles, they did not understand how His plan would come to fruition. They did not understand how the Gentiles would become "heirs together with Israel," "members together of one body," and "sharers together in the promise of Christ Jesus" (3:6) through the work of Jesus Christ.[6]

C. *Paul, the Servant of the Gospel Message* (Ephesians 3:8-13)

  1. Many translations break the first paragraph of chapter 3 between verses 6 and 7, but the original Greek includes verse 7 in the sentence that started in verse 2. Nonetheless, it makes sense to consider verse 7 as part of the

next paragraph because it introduces the next section that focuses on Paul's credentials for being given the "administration" of this gospel message.

a. Paul described his unworthiness for this responsibility, calling himself "less than the least of all the Lord's people" (3:8). He made up a word in the Greek that exaggerated the superlative, saying in essence, "I am the leastest of all God's people."[7]

b. He then repeated the description of his responsibility: to "preach to the Gentiles the unsearchable riches of Christ" (3:8) and to explain to everyone God's plan ("mystery") to unite Gentiles and Jews into one body (3:9).[8]

c. God initially kept the mystery hidden so that His plan would be "made known to the rulers and authorities in heavenly realms" (3:10) only when the Church came into being. These "rulers and authorities" were probably a reference to the evil and hostile spiritual beings that opposed God (3:10-11).

(1) The concept of God's plan being "made known" is not a reference to evangelism by the Church. Instead, it speaks of the creation of the Church as the means by which God unveiled the mystery, revealing His plan for ultimately defeating evil in the world.[9]

(2) In other words, Satan and the evil angels had no understanding of God's ultimate plan before the Church came into existence. They knew what the Old Testament said. They understood that a Savior would come, and they probably knew when and where He would come. But they had no idea God planned to establish the

Church and unite Jewish and Gentile believers into one body to praise and worship God. Perhaps God's delay in revealing this "mystery" was to preclude Satan from developing a different course of action for attacking Christ and the cross.[10]

2. In Ephesians 3:12, Paul reiterated the access we have to God that he mentioned in Ephesians 2:18. In chapter 3, though, his focus was slightly different. Not only does the united body of the Church have access to God, but such access is available "with freedom and confidence." Other versions refer to "boldness" and "confidence" (ESV, NASB, CSB).

> **How can we approach God with boldness and confidence?**

   a. Our access to God is only available "in Christ" and "through faith in Him."

   b. The Greek word for "freedom" is *parrasia*, which was used in classical Greek to refer to freedom of speech and the right to say everything one wished to say.[11] Typically, it referred to the fearlessness with which Christians could proclaim the gospel (see, e.g., Acts 4:31 and Ephesians 6:19-20). In this passage, though, Paul referred to the fearlessness with which believers can approach God.[12]

   (1) In other words, God has freely and fully given His children the grace of, not only *becoming* part of His family, but also the confidence of *knowing* they belong to Him and that they will always be a part of His family. This is a confidence that helps believers face the challenges of life, know-

ing that the final outcome of those challenges and of their lives will all bring glory to God.

(2) On the other hand, we must also be careful not to misunderstand or misapply this boldness. There are three mistakes Christians make when trying to act boldly before God:[13]

   (a) *Approaching God presumptuously and thinking He is at our command.* Boldness must always be coupled with reverence.

   (b) *Acting arrogantly and with an air of superiority.* Boldness must always be coupled with humility.

   (c) *Responding to God passively.* Boldness must always be coupled with action. Our confidence in God does not negate our responsibility to do good deeds and work for Him. Confidence empowers us to work. It should not lead us to inactivity.

c. Our access to God is expounded further in Hebrews 10:19-25. According to the writer of Hebrews, because we have such bold and confident access to God, we should …

(1) *"Draw near to God with a sincere heart"* (Hebrews 10:22). In other words, because of our access to God, we can walk and live daily in His presence.

   (a) We must approach Him "with a sincere heart and with the full assurance that faith brings" (Hebrews 10:22), i.e., an honest desire to live for Him and the total confidence we can trust Him in all situations.

(b) One of the reasons we can be so confident in God is because our hearts have been "sprinkled to cleanse us from a guilty conscience" (Hebrews 10:22). That means we are completely freed from guilt, not because of what we have done but because of what Christ has done for us.

(c) Another reason for our confidence is because our bodies have been "washed with pure water" (Hebrews 10:22). This is not a reference to baptism but a reference to a changed life, a life purified and cleansed by the work of Jesus Christ in us.

(2) *"Hold unswervingly to the hope we profess,* for he who promised is faithful" (Hebrews 10:23). In other words, we must practice what we preach and never deviate from the sound doctrines of our faith.

(3) *"Consider how we may spur one another on toward love and good deeds"* (Hebrews 10:24). How do we do this?

(a) First, we must not neglect meeting together (Hebrews 10:25). Here, again, is the emphasis on the importance of the Church.

(b) Second, we need to encourage one another (Hebrews 10:25) by worshipping together.

3. Paul closed this parenthetical interruption of his prayer with a final entreaty to his readers not to be discouraged because of his suffering on their behalf (3:13).

D. *The Reason for Paul's Prayer* **(Ephesians 3:14-15).** After the parenthetical thoughts in Ephesians 3:2-13, Paul returned to the prayer he started in Ephesians 3:1, expressing it again in a single Greek sentence that runs from verse 14 through verse 19.

1. Paul's prayer in Ephesians 1:15-23 was a prayer for understanding, enlightenment, and knowledge of our spiritual wealth. His prayer in Ephesians 3:14-19 is a prayer for power and enablement to use those riches. In other words, the first prayer is a prayer to *know* what we have; the second prayer is a prayer for the power to *use* what we have.[14] Consequently, this prayer provides the perfect transition and lead-in to the latter half of Paul's letter, which focuses on the practical applications of the truths described in the first half of the letter.

2. The prayer begins again (see Ephesians 3:1) with "for this reason" (3:14), referring to the truths Paul described at the end of chapter 2.[15] At the end of chapter 2, Paul described how the Gentiles and Jewish believers were united into one body—the Church—and how, as a result, the Gentiles became part of the "building blocks" of the Church.

    a. Thus, Paul's prayer was initiated by the truth of our identity as the dwelling place of God. The prayer, therefore, is a request for God to strengthen us so that we will use the power our status in Christ provides.

    b. Paul's reference to "every family in heaven and on earth" (3:14) was not a statement recognizing God as the spiritual father of every being in the universe—a new age concept. There are a couple of better ideas regarding what Paul meant by this phrase.

(1) One explanation is that Paul referred to the saints of all ages, both those who had died and were in heaven and those who were still alive on earth. As believers, our common spiritual father is God.[16]

(2) Another view is that Paul referred to God as the creator of all creatures, both angelic and human.[17]

E. **The Requests in Paul's Prayer** (Ephesians 3:16-19). Paul's prayer consisted of four requests, each one of which built on the previous one, making the prayer a "grand progression of enablement."[18]

1. FIRST REQUEST: INNER POWER FROM THE HOLY SPIRIT (3:16)

   a. Paul prayed that our "inner being" would be strengthened by power through the Holy Spirit (3:16).

   (1) What is the "inner being"? The inner being is the spiritual man as opposed to our materialistic natures. It refers to the moral part of man, including our reason, mind, and will. Thus Paul prayed for our characters to be strengthened and for us to be more spiritually minded in our motives and in the way we think and act.

   (2) How do we get that strength? It comes when we feed regularly on God's Word and seek the Spirit's will in our daily lives. We are strengthened as we exercise our spiritual muscles and yield to the Holy Spirit.

Ephesians 3:1-21

- b. Paul asked that this strength would come "out of [God's] glorious riches." He did not ask God to give us riches we do not already have. His prayer was for us to receive strength *out of* God's riches—a strength that empowers us to live our lives in a manner utilizing the spiritual wealth we already have in Christ.
- c. Notice, too, how often Paul prayed for the spiritual needs of others.[19] We need to be sensitive to and pray for the spiritual needs of others, not just for their physical needs.

2. SECOND REQUEST: INDWELLING OF CHRIST (3:17a)

- a. The purpose and result of being strengthened by the Holy Spirit is "so that Christ may dwell in your hearts through faith" (3:17a).
    - (1) The Holy Spirit's strength allows us to sense the presence of Jesus in our lives. This is a sensation that comes through our faith, not through our emotions.
    - (2) Another aspect of this passage is what it means for Christ to dwell in our hearts. This is the only place in Scripture in which the concept of Christ living in our hearts is used. Typically, the concept is that of the believer being "in Christ." But Paul's meaning here is to emphasize the need for our lives to be increasingly dominated and controlled by Christ.[20] He must be the center of our lives and the ruler of everything in our lives.
- b. The order of these first two requests seems to be reversed. We usually think about Christ dwelling in

our hearts first, and then power coming afterwards. But Paul's prayer was not for his readers to experience the indwelling of Christ for salvation because he was writing to people who were already Christians. Instead, he prayed for them to experience the reality of Christ's presence already within them.

(1) Thus, rather than talking about the *fact* of Christ's presence, Paul spoke about the *quality* of Christ's presence in a believer's life.[21]

(2) Pastor John MacArthur illustrates Paul's meaning by comparing the Christian life to a house. As Jesus comes to reside in the house, He must first clean it out. In the library, which represents the believer's mind, He throws out the trash and replaces it with the Word of God. In the dining room, He removes the sinful desires that form the appetite of the believer and stocks it with Christian virtues such as humility and love. He continues the same process throughout the house, cleaning out the clutter and dust of sin and folly so that He can settle in and be at home.[22] Once Christ is able to indwell our lives without the competition of sin as a roommate, we will experience the peace and power of Christ's presence in our lives.

c. The imagery of Christ indwelling our lives is a powerful one. Instead of Jesus being some small add-on to our lives whom we periodically think about or acknowledge when it fits our schedule, He is the authoritative presence in our lives who moves in and changes us. In fact, if we do not experience any change, we must seriously question whether Christ ever actually moved in.

3. THIRD REQUEST: KNOWLEDGE OF AN INCOMPREHENSIBLE LOVE (3:17b-19a)

   a. Inward strength through the Holy Spirit (3:16) leads to Christ being at home in our hearts (3:17a), which leads to our awareness of Christ's incomprehensible love for us and then our becoming rooted and grounded in that love (3:17b). Paradoxically, Paul prayed we would "know" Christ's unknowable love (3:19a). Clearly, Paul had in mind, not just an *intellectual* knowledge, but an *experiential* knowledge of Christ's love.

   b. What does it mean to be "rooted and established in love" (3:17)? It means to be totally immersed in Christ's love as the very basis of our being, which is the result of being empowered by the Holy Spirit and indwelt by Christ.

      (1) Once we are so immersed, we can then begin to grasp its vastness (i.e., its width, length, height, and depth) and "know this love that surpasses knowledge" (3:19).[23]

      (2) It is important to recognize that Paul was not speaking about knowing what kind of love we are supposed to have for Christ. He prayed that we would know "the love of Christ," that is, the love Christ has for us. The vastness of Christ's love for us is beyond anything the world is able to comprehend because the world only understands love that is based on attraction or on what it can get in return. Christ's love is an eternal love, given freely and unconditionally. Paul prayed that believers would truly grasp and know this unfathomable love from Christ.

4. FOURTH REQUEST: GOD'S FULLNESS (3:19b)

   a. The rooting and grounding of the love of Christ in our hearts leads to the filling of our lives with God's fullness.

   b. What does it mean to be filled with God's fullness?

   (1) Filling us is God's major goal—to fill His children with Himself, with everything He has and is, and to make us like Him. The magnitude of this goal is incomprehensible, and we can only begin to grasp what it entails when we consider the characteristics of God that He wants us to be filled with: His power, majesty, wisdom, love, holiness, mercy, patience, kindness, etc.

   > **What does it mean to be filled with God's fullness?**

   (2) Perhaps its meaning can best be understood if we think about what it means to be "filled with rage" or to be "filled with happiness." These phrases refer to being controlled or dominated by rage or happiness. Thus, to be filled with God is to be controlled and dominated by Him and His characteristics.

F. *The Conclusion of Paul's Prayer* **(Ephesians 3:20-21).** Paul concluded his prayer with a doxology of praise for God who is able to grant these amazing powers for which Paul prayed—yet, not only these powers, but even more—all for His glory.[24]

1. Only when we have been filled with God's fullness is God able to work in us in ways that go beyond our imagination. Otherwise, His work in us is limited if we are not strengthened by the Holy Spirit, indwelt by Christ, rooted and grounded in love, and filled with God's fullness.
2. Some commentators describe Ephesians 3:20 as a pyramid that reveals the progression of God's empowerment of us.

    a. The pyramid of progression looks like this:

God is *able* to do

God is able to do what we *ask*

God is able to do what we *imagine*

God is able to do *all* we ask or imagine

God is able to do *more* than we ask or imagine

God is able to do *immeasurably* more than we ask or imagine

      b. As MacArthur points out, most Christians believe God is able to do more than they can imagine, but few of them actually see Him do so because they fail to follow this progression of enablement in their lives.[25]

3. Once we become yielded to God so much that He is able to do more than we can imagine in our lives, then we become truly effective in our service for God and God is truly glorified (3:21).

Questions for Personal Reflection or Group Discussion

1. *Eph. 3:1:* What does Paul's description of himself as a "prisoner of Christ" teach us about the perspective we should have when we are going through trials?

2. *Eph. 3:2:* In what way are we also "administrators of God's grace"? What responsibility do we have in how we handle God's grace in our lives?

3. *Eph. 3:10:* How does God's plan to use the Church as a display of His wisdom to His enemies impact your view of the importance and role of the Church? How does it impact your faithfulness to the Church and your role in the Church?

4. *Eph. 3:12:* What does it mean that we can approach God "with freedom and confidence"?

    a. What does it *not* mean?

    b. What does Hebrews 10:22-25 teach us about how we can approach God boldly?

5. *Eph. 3:16:* What does it mean to be "strengthened with power" in our "inner being"? What should be the power-source of our lives?

6. *Eph. 3:17a:* What does it mean for Christ to "dwell in your hearts"? How does the indwelling of Christ in our lives affect our lives?

7. *Eph. 3:19a:* How can we know a "love that surpasses knowledge"? What is the difference between an *intellectual* knowledge and an *experiential* knowledge of God's love?

8. *Eph. 3:19b:* What does it mean to be filled with "the fullness of God"?

9. *Eph. 3:20:* How do you react to the "pyramid of progression" of God's empowerment? How does it impact your faith in God as you progressively move from believing that "God is able" to believing that "God is able to do immeasurably more than you ask or imagine"?

Chapter VII

Living in Unity
Ephesians 4:1-16

A. ***Walking in Unity* (Ephesians 4:1-6).** In chapters 4-6, Paul applied the doctrinal lessons of chapters 1-3 to the Christian's daily lifestyles. Ephesians 4:1 actually begins with another "therefore" ("then" in the New International Version). In other words, Paul drew the conclusion that, because of the spiritual blessings and riches we have from God, we should live our daily lives in a way that is "worthy of [our] calling" (4:1).

1. What does it mean to live "worthy of the calling you have received" (4:1)? Webster's Dictionary defines "worthy" as "having sufficient value." With that definition, the phrase suggests that our lives must reflect the value of the "calling [we] have received," referring to the salvation and spiritual blessings described in the first three chapters.

   > **Does your daily life reflect the value of the blessings and riches God has given you?**

   a. What difference would it make in our lives if we lived each moment in a manner worthy of being a recipient of God's salvation and spiritual blessings? In Hebrews 11:16, the writer said God was "not ashamed to be called" the God of the great men and women listed in the chapter because of the way they lived and exhibited their faith in God through both good and bad times. In other words, they lived "worthy of their calling." The challenge to believers today continues to be living in such a worthy manner so that God is not ashamed to be called our God.

    b. Another way to look at Ephesians 4:1 is to consider the translation in the King James Version: "walk worthy of your vocation." Paul described our Christian lives as a vocation. Imagine how differently we would treat our responsibilities to God if we actually viewed them to be our "vocation." Similarly, we might ask ourselves: what kind of performance review would we get in our "vocations" as Christians?

    c. Commentator Maxie Dunnam addresses the significance of this verse by highlighting Paul's use of "therefore" to start this section. According to Dunnam, the word highlights the primary difference between Christianity and other religions because it reveals that the Christian life is not one lived by our own resources in an attempt to be moral enough to please God. Instead, it is a "therefore walk." In other words, living moral and obedient lives for God is a response to what Christ has already done for us, not an attempt to earn His grace and mercy.[1]

2. Paul listed three characteristics of a worthy life:

    a. *Humility* (4:2a)

        (1) Perhaps the best description of humility is Christ's example described in Philippians 2:6-8:

"Who, being in very nature God, did not consider equality with God something to be used to his own advantage; rather, he made himself nothing by taking the very nature of a servant, being made in human likeness. And being found in appearance as a man, he humbled himself by becoming obedient to death—even death on a cross."

(2) To be humble, we must not be self-centered. As Paul further described it, we must "value others above yourselves, not looking to your own interests but each of you to the interests of the others" (Philippians 2:4).

b. *Gentleness* (4:2a)

(1) The Greek word for "gentle" (*prautetos*) is often translated "meek." Jesus mentioned this characteristic in His Sermon on the Mount, where He said, "Blessed are the meek, for they will inherit the earth" (Matthew 5:5). The Greek word used in the Beatitudes and in Ephesians 4:2 has the general meaning of submission. It pictures one who has become gentle of spirit, submissive, and tenderhearted. It is the word used to describe a wild horse after it has been broken. A broken wild horse is still strong and powerful, but when broken it puts its strength and power under the control of its rider. Thus, to be meek means to become submissive to God and to put all of our strengths, talents, intellect, desires, and will under His control.

(2) According to theologian W.E. Vine, "The common assumption is that when a man is meek it

is because he cannot help himself; but the Lord was 'meek' because he had the infinite resources of God at His command [as do we since we possess "every spiritual blessing"]. Described negatively, meekness is the opposite of self-assertiveness and self-interest; it is equanimity of spirit that is neither elated nor cast down, simply because it is not occupied with self at all."[2]

(3) In connection with our relationship with other believers, gentleness is characterized by "[carrying] each other's burdens" (Galatians 6:2). It means refusing to act harshly toward others.

c. *Patience and forbearance* (4:2b)

(1) Commentator Peter O'Brien defines "patience" this way: "'Patience' is that long-suffering which makes allowance for others' shortcomings and endures wrong rather than flying into a rage or desiring vengeance. It is a fruit of the Spirit (Galatians 5:22) and a necessary quality for maintaining right relationships within the body of Christ."[3]

(2) The patience we show others should be done "in love." In other words, our patience and forbearance are not simply acts of putting up with one another; they are acts performed because we love one another as fellow believers.

3. The three characteristics of a "worthy life" are essential characteristics for maintaining unity among the body of believers, which Paul commanded in Ephesians 4:3: "Make every effort to keep the unity of the Spirit through the bond of peace."

a. Paul's command has an air of urgency about it. The Greek word for "make every effort" (*spoudatsantes*) means to "use speed" and to be "prompt and earnest" about the effort. Paul commanded us not to be passive or quiet about the issue of unity among believers, merely waiting to see what occurs or letting whatever happens occur when unity is threatened. He told us to be passionate and watchful of our unity and to "make every effort" to preserve the unity created by the Holy Spirit.

b. Peace among believers is the glue—i.e., "the bond" (4:3)—that binds us together in unity.

c. Paul clarified the core truths that form the basis for Christian unity with a list of seven fundamental unity statements:[4]

  (1) We are "one body" (4:4), which is a reference to the Church as Christ's body (see Ephesians 1:23).

  (2) There is "one Spirit" (4:4), i.e., the Holy Spirit who brings unity to the body.

  (3) We have "one hope" (4:4) to which we were called, i.e., the confidence of our salvation and the fulfillment of God's promises to us.

  (4) The first three unities relate to the Holy Spirit. The next three relate to Jesus Christ, who is our "one Lord" (4:5).

  (5) Because there is only one Lord, we have only "one faith" (4:5), which is expressed by trusting solely in Jesus and believing the sound doctrines of the Christian faith.

(6) There is only "one baptism" (4:5), which refers to believers uniting in faith with Christ in a single relationship. That new relationship is symbolized by water baptism, which needs to be performed only one time as a symbol of our salvation.

(7) The last unity climaxes with "one God and Father" (4:6) who is transcendent over, and immanent in, all things.

(a) Paul described God as "over all," which refers to His transcendence, a characteristic highlighting God's distinctiveness and separateness from creation. The significance of this characteristic in God is that it means "[t]here is something higher than human beings. Good, truth, and value are not determined by the shifting flux of this world and human opinion. There is something which gives value to humankind from above."[5]

(b) God is also "through all and in all," a reference to His immanence, which means "God is present and active within his creation, and within the human race, even those members of it that do not believe in or obey him. His influence is everywhere. He is at work in and through natural processes."[6] In other words, God remains involved in creation, which is dependent on Him for its existence and sustenance. He is not a deistic god who is aloof and disinterested in His creation.[7]

B. *Walking in Maturity* **(Ephesians 4:7-16).** Paul shifted his thought from unity to diversity in verse 7 with the opening word, "But." His point was that unity does not mean uniformity, nor does unity eliminate individual responsibilities that each Christian has as a believer. Although we are to strive for unity, we must also understand that "each one of us" is different, with different gifts and responsibilities in the Church.

1. In Ephesians 4:7-11, Paul discussed another spiritual blessing God has given us: SPIRITUAL GIFTS.

   a. Paul called our spiritual gifts a "grace" from Christ, and he explained that each of our gifts was given to us "as Christ apportioned it" (4:7).[8] This special distribution of gifts by Christ emphasizes the fact that no gift is more important than another.

      (1) In verse 8, Paul quoted Psalm 68:18 to emphasize Jesus' sovereignty. His sovereignty is the reason He is authorized to apportion gifts as He sees fit (4:8).

         (a) Psalm 68 is one of the more difficult psalms to interpret. Commentators struggle to identify whether the entire psalm is a unified whole or a collection of different poems. Some believe the psalm may have been used when David moved the ark from the home of Obed-Edom to Jerusalem as recounted in 2 Samuel 6:12-19.[9] Regardless of its background, the psalm focuses

---

An Additional Spiritual Blessing from God (4:11-13)

Spiritual Gifts

generally on God's deliverance of His people from their enemies, whether physical or spiritual.[10]

(b) The context of Psalm 68:18 is God's victorious march to the top of Mount Sinai, where He led His captives as the conquering King and was honored by gifts from His people. The subsequent verses of the psalm describe how God's people shared in His victory.

　i. Paul modified the verse by changing the phrase "received gifts from men," as stated in Psalm 68:18, to "gave gifts to men." Commentator Derek Kidner explains Paul's rewording of the psalm as "[summarizing] rather than [contradicting] the psalm, whose next concern is with the blessings God dispenses."[11] In other words, Paul changed the wording of the psalm in order to apply its intended meaning, a meaning that distinguishes the nature of the Old Testament reality from the grace of the New Testament.

　ii. As William Barclay explains: "In the Old Testament the conquering king *demanded and received* gifts from men: in the New Testament the conqueror Christ *offers and gives* gifts to men. That is the essential difference between the two Testaments."[12]

(2) In a parenthetical aside (4:9-10), Paul explained that Psalm 68:18 implies God had to first descend "to the lower, earthly regions" (4:9), a reference to Jesus' incarnation and death, and then "ascended higher than all the heavens" (4:10), a reference to His resurrection and subsequent exaltation.[13] Paul's point, in other words, was that the power of the resurrection is what gives Christ the authority to distribute blessings and gifts however He sees fit.

b. Paul then described four spiritual gifts (or, more precisely, four spiritual roles that are gifts to the Church) (4:11).[14]

(1) *Apostles*

(a) An apostle is a messenger or person commissioned to fully represent the one who sent him.[15] In the historic context of Paul's day, Paul most likely referred to the twelve men chosen as Christ's apostles and who helped establish the early Church.

(b) While there are no longer any such apostles today, the role of the apostle most closely corresponds to today's missionaries who teach the foundations of truth in new parts of the world and help start new congregations of believers, much as the twelve apostles did.

(2) *Prophets*

(a) A prophet is one who speaks for God and unveils the mind of God. The gift of a prophet differs from that of an apostle in that the apostle authoritatively declares the truth while the prophet interprets the word and explains it in a clear and compelling way.

(b) The word "prophet" comes from a root word and prefix meaning "to shine before." This meaning is reflected in 2 Peter 1:19, which says, "We also have the prophetic message as something completely reliable, and you will do well to pay attention to it, *as to a light shining in a dark place,* until the day dawns and the morning star rises in your hearts" (emphasis added).

(3) *Evangelists*

(a) An evangelist is one who can communicate the gospel in relevant, compelling terms to non-Christians. An evangelist has the ability to explain clearly the why and how of Jesus' redemptive work.

(b) This gift is different from the requirement that all of us be witnesses. As witnesses we are called simply to share with others what has happened to us. No special gift is necessary in order to perform the role of a witness.

(4) *Pastor/Teachers*. The pastor/teacher is one who maintains the body by feeding it the Word, calling for renewal and repentance, and encouraging growth through ministry and fellowship.

c. It is important to recognize that these gifts are not made available only to clergy. These gifts are distributed both to clergy and non-clergy.

   (1) Football has been described as "eleven men on a field in desperate need of rest, surrounded by fifty thousand people in the stands in desperate need of exercise." Pastor Ray Stedman suggests that the local church often works in a similar manner with the ministerial staff doing the ministry while the congregation spectates. God's plan for the church, though, is different. God designed it so that every member in the church is a minister and responsible for performing the ministry.[16]

   (2) How can you learn what your gifts are?

      (a) Two ways are the most effective. The first is to begin doing and serving, which is the best way to determine your gifts. The second is the affirmation of others.

      (b) Snodgrass, however, points out that Scripture never commands us to identify our gifts. He says Scripture commands us to serve and build up the church by doing whatever the Spirit has called us to do. Rather than spending our time *identifying* what our gifts are, we should instead be busy *being* a gift to the body of Christ.[17]

> **Scripture never commands us to *identify* our gifts. It simply commands us to *be* a gift by serving the body of Christ.**

d. What are the purposes of these spiritual roles in the Church? Their purposes are two-fold:

   (1) First, the roles are needed "to equip [God's] people for works of service" (4:12). The job of our church leaders is to build up and equip the rest of God's people to perform ministry. It is not the responsibility of the ministers to do everything in the church. Each member in the body of believers is expected to perform "works of service" that help to build up the Church body.

   (2) The second purpose of these spiritual roles is to build up the Church so that it attains unity and maturity (4:13). In fact, we must continue our "works of service," for as long as it takes, or "until" the church reaches complete unity and maturity as measured by Christ's standards.

2. Paul then described the result of maturity in the Christian life (4:14-16). He listed five results, all of which are evidences of spiritual maturity in our own lives. In fact, when reading through this passage, believers can conduct a self-analysis of their own growth in maturity. As a believer you might ask yourself, "Am I living a life of …"

   a. *Stability* (4:14). Paul compared immature believers to "infants" who are thrown around by the prevailing waves and winds of the philosophies and opinions of those trying to manipulate us to turn away from the truth of God's Word and teachings. Maturity helps us not be easily confused by false teachings and the latest fads.

b. *Loving communication of the truth* (4:15a).

   (1) Instead of being crafty people speaking false doctrine, we need to be loving people who "[speak] the truth."

   (2) The Greek word translated "speaking the truth" is actually one word written in the present participle form (*aletheuontes*) that literally means "truthing." By turning the noun into a verb, Paul emphasized that truth is something a person *does*, not just something one *speaks*.[18] This idea is illustrated by a story Pastor H.A. Ironside tells about a conversation between two friends. Responding to a question asking what he thought was the best translation of the New Testament, one of the young men answered without hesitation, "'My mother's.' His friend said, 'Your mother's! I didn't know she was a scholar. Did she translate the New Testament?' 'My mother was not a scholar, she could not read a word of Greek, but she translated the New Testament into her beautiful life, and that made more of an impression on me than anything else I have ever known.'"[19]

c. *Growth to maturity* (4:15b). As we "[speak] the truth in love," we grow in spiritual maturity "in every respect," both as individuals and as a body of believers.

d. *Unity in spirit and attitude with other Christians* (4:16a). As a united Church, we are "joined and held together by every supporting ligament," which refers to every individual member doing his or her responsibility and using his or her gifts.

e. *Responsibility* (4:16b). Each part of the Church must "[do] its work." Every member must do what they are called to do in the Church if the Church is going to grow and flourish.

Ephesians 4:1-16

Questions for Personal Reflection or Group Discussion

1. *Eph. 4:1:* What does it mean to live "worthy of the calling you have received"? Does your daily life reflect the value of the blessings and riches God has given you?

2. *Eph. 4:2:* What are the three characteristics of a worthy life? How is each characteristic displayed in our lives?

3. *Eph. 4:3-6:* How does Paul describe the unity that exists among believers? What is the bond that holds our unity together?

4. *Eph. 4:7:* What is the difference between unity and uniformity? In what ways is each of us different from other believers?

5. *Eph. 4:7-10:* What act of Christ grants Him the authority and right to distribute spiritual gifts to believers?

6. *Eph. 4:11:* Describe how each of the spiritual gifts listed by Paul are displayed in the Church today?

7. *Eph. 4:12-13:* What are the purposes of spiritual gifts?

8. *Eph. 4:14-16:* What are some of the measurements of spiritual maturity in believers and in the Church?

Chapter VIII

Living in Purity
Ephesians 4:17-5:2

A. *Out With the Old; In With the New* **(Ephesians 4:17-24).** In the first half of Ephesians 4 (verses 1-16), Paul urged the Ephesians to live in unity. In the second half of chapter 4, he exhorted them to live daily lives of purity, using language that emphasized the importance and urgency of his exhortation ("I tell you this, and insist on it in the Lord" (4:17)). The passage compares the way we are to live with the way we are not to live, i.e., "as the Gentiles do" (4:17). Even though Paul's audience was primarily a Gentile one, he referred here to their prior lives as unconverted pagans and the current environment of paganism that surrounded them. He urged them to "live," or "walk" (ESV, NASB, CSB), differently than unbelievers do.

1. In Ephesians 4:17, Paul described the godless world as people who live "in the futility of their thinking." What does that mean?

   a. The Greek word for "futility" (*mataioteti*) refers to the emptiness and worthlessness of their thoughts on spiritual or moral things. The clause could also be translated as those "whose thoughts are worthless," or "what they think has no value," or "what they think means nothing."[1] Paul described it further in verse 18 as "ignorance," speaking of their obliviousness to God and to the truth.

b. Paul explained that the futility of pagan thinking results in and is exhibited in several ways:

   (1) *Darkened Understanding.* "They are darkened in their understanding" (4:18). The Greek tense Paul used with this clause emphasized that this darkness is not temporary but one that persists in the lives of those without Christ. They are completely "incapable of grasping the truth of God and his gospel."[2] The minds of those who do not know Christ are and remain in the dark.

   (2) *Separation from God.* They are "separated from the life of God" (4:18), referring to the eternal life God gives to His children. In other words, they are spiritually dead, and the fault is their own doing because of "the hardening of their hearts" (4:18) that comes from an obstinate and persistent rejection of God and His will. Such continued rejection of God progressively hardens a person's conscience until it becomes no longer able to convict the person of sin.[3]

      (a) Paul described their hardened hearts as "having lost all sensitivity" (4:19a). The phrase in its literal sense referred to calloused skin that no longer feels pain. Of course, Paul's use of it was meant in the spiritual sense, referring to the lost ability to feel shame or guilt or to exhibit self-control.[4]

      (b) The phrase implies a warning we all should heed. We must be careful not to become "insensitive." Sometimes sin can be so prevalent around us we soon fail to notice it, even in our own lives.

(3) *Sinful Indulgence*. With hardened hearts and insensitive consciences, those without Christ abandon themselves to "sensuality," "every kind of impurity," and "greed" (4:19b). One commentator expresses Paul's description of human sinfulness in formulaic terms: "Darkened minds + darkened hearts = darkened behavior."[5]

(a) "Sensuality" is a Greek word (*aselgeia*) often translated as "licentiousness," "lasciviousness," or "debauchery." The Christian Standard Bible uses "promiscuity." It refers to "unrestrained living"[6] and a total disregard for public decency.[7]

(b) "Impurity" was often associated with unrestrained sexual behavior, but Paul probably contemplated conduct beyond only sexual behavior since he referred to *"every kind* of impurity" (4:19 emphasis added).

(c) "Greed" referred to a constant craving and lust for more of that which is evil.

2. On the opposite spectrum from such an evil world are believers. As Christians we have been called to the Truth, which is Christ Jesus, who calls us to a renewed life and attitude exemplified by righteous acts and holy lives (4:20-24).

a. Followers of Christ are taught to "put off your old [selves]" (4:22). This is a reference to the old ways of the pagan life Paul described in the preceding verses, calling it a life that was "being corrupted by its deceitful desires" (4:22b).

b. It is not enough simply to quit being corrupt and deceived, but we must also start living "like God in true righteousness and holiness" (4:24). In other words, not only should we "put off [the] old self" (4:22), but we must also "put on the new self" (4:24).

c. Such a change in our lives and actions comes from being "made new in the attitude [some translations say "spirit" (ESV, NASB, CSB)] of [our] minds" (4:23). In other words, we cannot put on a new life without experiencing the inward renewal that the Holy Spirit accomplishes in us. It is not enough for us to change our beliefs and opinions; we must also change our lifestyles, our habits, and our character.

(1) Unlike the concepts of "putting off the old" and "putting on the new" (both of which terms are expressed as aorist infinitives that depict completed past actions), being "made new" uses a present infinitive, suggesting ongoing activity. The renewal of our inward minds and spirits is an ongoing process that occurs as we yield to God on a daily basis.[8]

(2) What must we do to allow the Holy Spirit to renew our spirits and minds? There are three things we should do:[9]

(a) *Keep our minds focused on those things that are consistent with godliness and Christlikeness.* Paul said, "Whatever is true, whatever is noble, whatever is right, whatever is pure, whatever is lovely, whatever is admirable—if anything is excellent or praiseworthy—

think about such things. Whatever you have learned or received or heard from me, or seen in me—put it into practice" (Philippians 4:8-9).

(b) *Avoid the world's way of thinking, but think instead with a transformed manner.* As Paul told the Romans, "Do not conform to the pattern of this world, but be transformed by the renewing of your mind. Then you will be able to test and approve what God's will is—his good, pleasing and perfect will" (Romans 12:2).

(c) *Study God's Word.* Paul encouraged Timothy, "Continue in what you have learned and have become convinced of, because you know those from whom you learned it, and how from infancy you have known the Holy Scriptures, which are able to make you wise for salvation through faith in Christ Jesus" (2 Timothy 3:14-15).

(3) The lesson in these verses is that we as believers must live differently from the world and society around us.

(a) The first area in which we must be different from the world is, according to Paul, our thought-life. In other words, a believer's way of thinking, his philosophies and values, and his beliefs and opinions should reflect the philosophy and values of God. This is one of the most fundamental differences between the Christian and the world. If a Christian wants to follow Christ, his entire way of thinking must be made new, thus transforming his outlook and approach to life in a way that is diametrically opposite to the world's mindset.[10]

(b) In order to live such a different lifestyle, it is not only essential to be obedient to God but also to enlighten a darkened world with the Truth of Jesus Christ. We must exhibit to the world a whole new set of values and ways of thinking. If we fail to do so, we will not be able to help those who are lost in the darkness of the world's philosophies.[11]

B. *Off With the Old; On With the New* **(Ephesians 4:25-5:2).** After describing our need to stop living the old life of our pagan past and to start living our new life in Christ, Paul then provided specific examples of how we can do that in our daily lives by "putting off" the old life practices and "putting on" characteristics of the new life.

1. OFF WITH FALSEHOOD – ON WITH SPEAKING TRUTH (4:25). We must put off lying and put on speaking truthfully to one another.[12]

    a. It is significant that Paul's first exhortation for living the new life centers on the integrity of our words. The speech of believers is a frequent concern in Scripture. In fact, in Proverbs 6:16, lying is listed as one of the seven things God hates.

    b. The reason we need to speak the truth is because "we are all members of one body" (4:25b). In other words, truth is necessary in order to maintain unity within the body since lying destroys trust and without trust there can be no unity.

(1) Even so-called "small" fibs we tell in order to spare someone's feelings often result in mistrust. As I wrote in an earlier book, "Deceptive speech undermines people's trust in us and destroys relationships, as pointed out in a study published in 2001. The study examined the idea that deception is necessary to maintain a good relationship with those we love. The study found, though, that deception, including the 'white lies' told to protect one's partner, led to higher suspicions and lower trust between the partners."[13]

(2) Sam Harris, an author and neuroscientist, compares lying to toxic waste. Both, he says, harm everyone to whom it spreads.[14]

2. OFF WITH ANGER – ON WITH RECONCILIATION (4:26-27). We must put off festering anger and put on early resolution of our conflicts with others.

   a. In verse 26, Paul quoted Psalm 4:4, which says, "Be angry, and do not sin" (ESV). The gist of the psalm and Paul's command was not to let anger against others fester and linger in our lives and minds and thereby allow bitterness to arise. In fact, Paul encouraged believers to resolve their anger before sundown (4:26b). This is probably more of a proverbial saying rather than an actual deadline for dealing with anger, but its meaning is clear: we must not let our anger at someone, regardless of how justified, continue for so long that it becomes a brooding bitterness against that person.[15]

   b. The reason we must learn to reconcile quickly with those who anger us is because a lingering anger is a way for Satan to gain "a foothold" in our lives and in our churches (4:27). Satan often uses prolonged, unresolved anger to exploit the strains between people in order to destroy their unity and love for one another.

3. OFF WITH STEALING – ON WITH WORKING HARD AND SHARING (4:28). We must put off stealing and put on hard work. Interestingly, Paul said the purpose of our work is so that we have something to "share with those in need" (4:28). What a different view of work than what the world has! In other words, believers should have the perspective that their jobs and careers are not solely to provide for their own needs and wants or to satisfy their personal drives and ambitions, but instead we work in order to have enough to help others who are unable to care for themselves.

4. OFF WITH UNWHOLESOME TALK – ON WITH ENCOURAGING TALK (4:29-30). We must put off "unwholesome talk" and put on encouraging talk.

   a. Paul returned to the importance of a believer's speech but moved beyond the problem of lying. He encouraged the Ephesians not to "let any unwholesome talk come out of your mouths" (4:29). The Greek word for "unwholesome" (*sapros*) means "rotten" and was used when speaking of rotten fish or fruit.[16] In other words, unwholesome speech smells like rotten fish! This includes dirty words and jokes, negativism, prejudice, slander, gossip, etc. Nothing we say should be harmful. Jesus underscored this command when He said, "I tell you that everyone will have to give account on the day of judgment for every empty word they have spoken. For by your words you will be acquitted, and by your words you will be condemned" (Matthew 12:36-37).[17]

b. Instead of using our words to harm others, we should speak in ways that are "helpful for building others up according to their needs" (4:29) and for their benefit. "Someone offered good advice on how to check ourselves before we speak ill about another person by asking ourselves three questions: Is what I am about to say true; is it necessary; and is it kind? If the answer to any one of those questions is 'no,' then it is a good time to follow the advice that Bambi's friend, Thumper, received from his father: 'If you can't say somethin' nice, don't say nothin' at all.'"[18]

	"Put off your old self" (4:22)	**"Put on the new self" (4:24)**
4:25	Put Off Falsehood	Put On Speaking Truth
4:26	Put Off Anger	Put On Reconciliation
4:28	Put Off Stealing	Put On Working Hard and Sharing
4:29-30	Put Off Unwholesome Talk	Put On Encouraging Talk
4:31-32	Put Off Malice and Hatefulness	Put On Kindness and Compassion

c. The reason we need to be careful with our words is because it "grieves the Holy Spirit of God" (4:30).

(1) Grieving is a love-related word. You can only grieve a person who loves you. How do we grieve the Holy Spirit? We grieve Him when we have division with other people and hurt those

whom He also loves, including when we do these things with the use of harmful words.

(2) A Christian who uses foul language grieves the Holy Spirit because such language is a denial of His presence and sanctifying work within the believer.[19] As James said, "Out of the same mouth come praise and cursing. My brothers and sisters, this should not be" (James 3:10).

5. OFF WITH MALICE AND HATEFULNESS – ON WITH KINDNESS AND COMPASSION (4:31-32). We must put off "every form of malice" and put on kindness, compassion, and forgiveness.

   a. Paul returned to the idea of anger at the end of his list. In fact, the terms he used in verse 31 suggested a progression in intensity from an inner bitterness to a raging anger and ultimately loud confrontation and abuse.[20] Each word Paul used carries with it an increasingly darker meaning:

   (1) Bitterness, i.e., an irritable state of mind that makes a person perpetually feel and act harshly and hatefully toward other people. The Greek word (*pikria*) referred to an acrid taste or smell that was bitterly pungent and irritating to a person's eyes and nose. An acrid mindset also becomes bitterly pungent and irritating within our own spirits and ultimately to those around us.

   (2) Rage, i.e., an explosive, unrestrained temper.

   (3) Anger, i.e., an inner desire to hurt others or to get revenge. The Greek term for "anger" (*orgē*) differs from the earlier word translated "rage" (*thumos*). *Orgē* is a slower, simmering, and abid-

Ephesians 4:17-5:2

ing anger, while *thumos* ("rage") arises suddenly and passionately and subsides just as suddenly.²¹

(4) Brawling, i.e., a loud, confrontational attitude toward others to embarrass or intimidate them.

(5) Slander, i.e., defamatory speech that injures another's reputation, including gossip. The word for slander (*blasphemia*) is the same Greek word that is often translated "blasphemy" and used to refer to speech that defames God.

(6) Malice, i.e., the general quality of depravity and having a bad heart. It is used in verse 31 as the catch-all term that describes the root of all the other listed vices.

b. Instead of these kinds of attitudes and actions, we should show kindness, compassion, and forgiveness to others just as Christ did for us (4:32).

6. IMITATE GOD (5:1-2). Paul concluded this section with a final admonition that summed up his teachings in this section: "Follow God's example" (5:1), or as other translations put it, "Be imitators of God" (ESV, NASB, CSB).

a. That exhortation along with the command to "walk in the way of love" (5:2) wraps all of the specific statements Paul made into a single goal for each of us: Imitate God by loving others as Christ loved us.

b. We can do that (1) by controlling our minds to ensure we think with a transformed mind, not a worldly mind, (2) by controlling our tongues to ensure we always speak truthfully, encouragingly, and compassionately, (3) by controlling our emotions to ensure we do not become angry and bitter

105

in our attitudes, and (4) by controlling our actions to ensure we work hard and share with those in need.

Questions for Personal Reflection or Group Discussion

1. *Eph. 4:17-19:* What did Paul mean when he described pagan people as living "in the futility of their thinking"? What three ways did Paul say nonbelievers exhibit the "futility of their thinking"?
2. *Eph. 4:22-24:* What must we do to allow the Holy Spirit to renew our spirits and minds?
3. *Eph. 4:25-32:* Think about each of the examples Paul provided of what we need to "put off" from our old lives before Christ and what we need to "put on" in their place. Which of them speak to you the most, and why?
    a. Falsehood – Truth
    b. Anger – Reconciliation
    c. Stealing – Working hard and sharing
    d. Unwholesome talk – Encouraging talk
    e. Malice and Hatefulness – Kindness and Compassion
4. *Eph. 5:1-2:* What areas of your life do you need to work on in order to be a better follower, or imitator, of God's example?

Chapter IX

Living as Children of Light
Ephesians 5:3-21

A. *Living as a Light of Purity* **(Ephesians 5:3-14).** In Ephesians 4:1, Paul told us to "live a life worthy of [our] calling;" in Ephesians 4:17, he told us not to "live as the Gentiles do;" and, in Ephesians 5:2, he said to "walk [or live] in the way of love." Now, in this Scripture passage, Paul commanded us to "live as children of light" (5:8), and he explained how we do that in a couple of ways. The first way is to live as a light of purity, continuing the theme of purity he covered in Ephesians 4:17-5:2.

1. AVOID THE DARKNESS OF SEXUAL IMMORALITY (5:3-7). Paul's primary focus in this passage with respect to living as "children of light" is for believers to avoid sexual immorality. Among Christians, there should not even be "a hint of sexual immorality" simply because it is improper for people who are holy (5:3).

    a. Paul said we must avoid any kind of improper sexual activity, which he described from three aspects—the same three aspects he used in Ephesians 4:19 to describe the sins of pagan Gentiles.

    (1) "Immorality" (*porneia*) refers to any kind of sexual misconduct, including incest, adultery,

THE CHRISTIAN WALK		
Where the NIV uses the word "live" in Ephesians, other translations use "walk." Throughout the letter, Paul admonished believers to walk as believers, describing that walk in a variety of ways.	
Ephesians 4:1	Walk in a manner worthy of your calling
Ephesians 4:1	Don't walk like the Gentiles do
Ephesians 5:2	Walk in the way of love
Ephesians 5:8	Walk like children of light
Ephesians 5:15	Walk wisely, making the most of every opportunity

sex outside marriage, and sexual relations with prostitutes.[1]

(2) "Impurity" (*akatharsia*) refers to filth and obscenity. This word refers to things such as pornography, immoral thoughts, fantasies, and other sexual corruption.

(3) "Greed" (*pleonexia*) refers to covetousness generally, but in this context, more specifically to sexual lust. Later, Paul referred to the greedy person as "an idolater" (5:5).

b. Not only are we not to be involved in sexual misconduct, we should not even be involved in discussing sexual activity in an improper way, including "obscenity, foolish talk or coarse joking" (5:4). This does not mean that sex is improper and, therefore, should never be discussed. The Bible does not require believers to be prudes. It simply tells us to avoid discussing sex in an immoral way or with a focus on its improper use.

(1) "Obscenity" refers to any form of degrading and disgraceful talk. It is the same exhortation Paul made in Colossian 3:8 where he commanded his readers to avoid "filthy language from your lips."

(2) "Foolish talk" translates the Greek word *morologia*, from which we get our word "moron." It consists of silly, foolish speech that we often refer to as a "dirty mouth."

(3) "Coarse joking" refers to dirty jokes. It is the kind of joking that turns anything a person says or does into something nasty with sexual innuendo.

(4) All of these terms command us not to have dirty minds or to be vulgar in our speech. Instead, our talk should consist of "thanksgiving" (5:4).

c. In fact, persons who live this kind of lifestyle are not Christians. As Paul put it, they have no "inheritance in the kingdom of Christ and of God" (5:5). Paul was not saying a believer who commits any of these sins will lose his salvation. His point is that those whose regular lifestyle is lived in such a manner provide evidence that they are not part of the kingdom of God to begin with. As commentator Peter

O'Brien puts it, those who live "in slavery to their sexual appetites are surely excluded from the rule of Christ and God."[2]

(1) Paul made a unique reference to the kingdom of God when he described it in a dual manner, calling it "the kingdom of Christ and of God" (5:5).

   (a) In his other writings, Paul referred either to the "kingdom of God" or the "kingdom of Christ," using different terms to describe the spiritual kingdom from different perspectives. Typically, the kingdom of God refers to the future and eternal kingdom, and the kingdom of Christ speaks of the present spiritual kingdom on earth. Eventually, the two kingdoms will merge, according to 1 Corinthians 15:24.

   (b) Paul's reference in Ephesians to the kingdom as both "of Christ and of God" highlighted Paul's emphasis that an immoral lifestyle precludes a person from both the present kingdom of Christ and the eternal kingdom of God.[3]

(2) Not only must we avoid such behavior, we must also be careful not to be deceived by people's excuses for living this way (5:6). A child of God simply cannot live this way, nor should he become partnered up with those who do (5:7).

   (a) We are not being told to avoid all contact with such people, but we are warned not to become closely associated with them in a manner that causes us to participate in their immorality.[4]

    (b) Paul's main point was not about avoiding non-believers for fear their sins would defile us. Instead, Paul wanted to be sure that the light of the gospel message which believers are expected to convey would not be overshadowed or dimmed by the acts of darkness.

2. LIVE IN THE LIGHT OF RIGHTEOUSNESS (5:8-14). The reason we should not live in such an immoral manner is because, once we become believers, we are no longer part of the darkness but have become "light in the Lord" (5:8). Thus, we not only should avoid the darkness of immorality, but we should instead live in the light of righteousness.

    a. As "children of light," we are to bear "the fruit of the light," which consists of "goodness, righteousness, and truth" (5:9).

    b. Paul specifically defined the life of a "child of light" as the process of "[finding] out [or "discerning" (ESV), or "trying to learn" (NASB)] what pleases the Lord" (5:10). In other words, the goal for our lives and actions, both individually and corporately as a Church, must always be to do that which pleases Christ.

        (1) One of the things that pleases God is to live so that we not only avoid the "fruitless deeds of

darkness" (5:11a) but we expose them by the light of our lives (5:11b-13).

(a) This is similar to what Paul described in Philippians 2:15-16, where he said we are to be "blameless and pure, children of God without fault in a crooked and depraved generation, in which you shine like stars in the universe as you hold out the word of life."

(b) Jesus also called us "the light of the world" and told us to "let [our] light shine before others, that they may see [our] good deeds and glorify [our] Father in heaven" (Matthew 5:14-16).

(2) Paul explained that the result of living in this way is we help "illuminate" the way for others to Christ, leading them to repentance ("Wake up, O sleeper ...") and drawing them to salvation ("... rise from the dead, and Christ will shine on you") (5:14).[5]

B. *Living as a Light of Wisdom* **(Ephesians 5:15-21)**

1. In Ephesians 5:15, Paul summarized this next section with a warning—"Be very careful, then, how you live"—as he continued his description of what it means to live a life "worthy of the calling you have received" (4:1) and to live "as children of light" (5:8). The second way we do so is to live as a light of wisdom. In particular, we are to live carefully, circumspectly, and with an awareness of the effects the way we live has on ourselves, God, and others.

2. Paul further explained what such a careful and circumspect life looks using three "not ... but" contrasts.

   a. *Not Unwise, But Wise* (5:15b-16). First, we must be careful to live "not as unwise but as wise" people (5:15b), meaning our lives are to be lived in such a way as to reflect the wisdom of God, not the foolishness of men. Such wise living requires us to make "the most of every opportunity" (5:16), or, as other translations put it, make the best use "of the time" (ESV, NASB, CSB).

   > **How do we live wisely?**

   (1) As believers, we should not waste the opportunities we have to serve God. Squandering our opportunities to serve God because we are busy with the trivial matters of the world or indifferent to our responsibilities to God is spiritual foolishness.

   (2) One of the reasons we need to use our time wisely is because "the days are evil" (5:16). In other words, we cannot let our lives be wasted for a single moment because evil is so prominent in the world.

   b. *Not Foolishly, But Understanding God's Will* (5:17). A wise lifestyle "understands what the Lord's will is" (5:17).

   (1) Our focus as believers who are trying to live wisely is to follow God's will, not foolishly follow the will of men. This verse is not speaking of specific guidance from God about precise as-

pects of our lives, but applies to a general reliance on Him in the way we live and the decisions we make each day, having a basic understanding of God's will for the world and for our lives.

(2) This type of understanding of God's will comes from regularly reading the Word of God and prayerfully meditating on its meaning and application in our lives.

c. *Not Drunk With Wine, But Filled with the Spirit* (5:18-21).[6] A wise lifestyle is also one that is "filled with the Spirit" (5:18).

(1) What does it mean to be "filled with the Spirit"?

(a) First, it is important to understand what the term does *not* mean. It does not mean ...[7]

i. A second blessing of advanced spirituality after salvation;

ii. The indwelling of the Spirit (which already occurs for believers at salvation);

iii. A progressive process of receiving the Spirit by degrees (because believers receive all of the Spirit at salvation);[8]

iv. The baptism of the Spirit (which also occurs for believers at salvation);

v. The sealing of the Spirit (which, again, occurs at salvation).

(b) To be filled with the Spirit can best be described with three illustrations:[9]

i. Being filled by the Spirit means to be *guided by* the Spirit, like a ship driven by the wind filling its sails. When we are filled with the Spirit, the Spirit drives us along as His spiritual guidance fills our lives.

ii. Being filled by the Spirit means to be *permeated with* the Spirit, like salt permeating meat to flavor and preserve it. When we are filled with the Spirit, the Spirit permeates our lives to such an extent our thoughts, words, and actions reflect His presence.

iii. Being filled by the Spirit means to be under the *total control and domination* of the Spirit. When we are filled with the Spirit we are totally controlled by His desires and passions, like the movements of a glove are controlled by the hand inside it.

(c) All of these illustrations can be contrasted against actual drunkenness. When a person is drunk on wine, the wine moves him along, permeates his thoughts and actions, and totally controls and dominates him.

(2) There are three results to being filled with the Spirit:

    (a) We sing—to one another and to the Lord—because of joy in our hearts (5:19).

    (b) We give thanks to God—always—for everything (5:20).

    (c) We submit to one another as a way to honor Christ in reverence and fear (5:21).[10]

(3) So how can we be filled with the Spirit?

    (a) It is a continual process involving submission, confession, repentance, and faith. We must daily submit our wills to the guidance of the Holy Spirit, confess and repent of sin in our lives, and trust Him by faith.

    (b) In Colossians 3:16, Paul encouraged the Colossians to "let the message of Christ dwell among you richly." When we do so, Paul said the result is singing, gratitude, and acting in the name of the Lord. These are the same results that come from being filled with the Spirit. Consequently, when we consider the teachings of these two Scripture passages together it is clear that, in order to be filled with the Spirit, we must also be filled with the Word of God.[11]

Questions for Personal Reflection or Group Discussion

1. *Eph. 5:3-6:* Paul said that believers should not have "even a hint of sexual immorality" in their lives. Why are we to avoid such immorality?
2. *Eph. 5:7:* How do you reconcile Paul's warning not to "be partners" with those who are disobedient to God with the viewpoint that we need to be friends with sinners in order to have the opportunity to share Christ with them?
3. *Eph. 5:10:* How does Paul express the goal for our lives?
4. *Eph. 5:16:* What does it mean to "make the most of every opportunity"? How does that constitute wise living?
5. *Eph. 5:18:* What does it mean to "be filled with the Spirit"? Why does Paul contrast being filled with the Spirit with being drunk?
6. *Eph. 5:18:* What must we do to be "filled with the Spirit"?

Chapter X

Living in Mutual Submission
Ephesians 5:21-6:9

A. *Submitting to One Another* **(Ephesians 5:21).** The command to "submit to one another" in Ephesians 5:21 serves as both a concluding remark to the preceding verses and an introduction to the next section. Paul had been talking about living in unity and in purity, but beginning in verse 21 he turned his focus to relationships between believers.[1] In verse 21, he summarized the essential ingredient for all successful Christian relationships and the remedy for all conflicts: submission to one another.

   1. The world resolves conflict by the assertion of power. For the Christian, though, conflict resolution comes at the individual level through submission.

   2. What is the meaning of "submission"?

      a. Submission is an attitude of yielding to another person as an act of self-denial rather than self-fulfillment. It means putting other people's interests above our own rather than insisting that we must have our own way in all matters.[2]

      b. The irony of being submissive to the needs of other people is that such submission leads to a greater sense of fulfillment in our lives. Stedman calls this truth a great paradox: the more we try to fulfill our own lives the emptier we become. As he points out, when people are focused on getting want they want in order to be fulfilled, the end result is frequently disappointment. When we give ourselves to others, we usually find more satisfaction in life.[3]

3. What is the reason for submitting? We are told to submit to one another out of "reverence for Christ" (5:21b).

   a. As Christians, every relationship we have includes another Person: Jesus. Conflicts between Christians are not simply husband vs. wife, or parent vs. child, or employee vs. employer. The issue in Christian conflict is not "what I want vs. what you want." The real issue is "what does Christ want?"

   b. In Ephesians 5:22-6:9, Paul applied the principle of submission to various Christian relationships in what are commonly called "house codes."[4] In each instance, Christ is at the center of the relationship and the key to resolving any conflict in the relationship.[5]

> **Christ is at the center of every relationship and is the key to resolving any conflict in the relationship.**

     (1) Ephesians 5:22: "Wives, submit to your husbands *as to the Lord.*"

     (2) Ephesians 5:25: "Husbands, love your wives, just *as Christ* loved the church …."

     (3) Ephesians 6:1: "Children, obey your parents *in the Lord* …."

(4) Ephesians 6:4: "Fathers, do not exasperate your children; instead, bring them up in the training and instruction *of the Lord.*"

(5) Ephesians 6:5: "Slaves, obey your earthly masters ..., just as you would *obey Christ.*"

(6) Ephesians 6:9: "And masters, treat your slaves in the same way, ... since you know that *he who is both their Master and yours* is in heaven ...."

B. *Submitting in Marriage* (Ephesians 5:22-33)

1. THE WIFE'S RESPONSIBILITY TO SUBMIT (5:22-24). In the marriage relationship, the wife is told to submit to the headship of the husband as an act of submission to the Lord.[6] This is not a command to "obey" the husband, but it is an act of yielding to the one with responsibility for the family just as the Church submits to the authority of Jesus Christ (5:23-24).

   a. Submission by the wife to the headship of the husband does not mean the wife is subservient or inferior to the husband. Instead it means the wife voluntarily places herself under the spiritual leadership of the husband and willingly adapts and adjusts herself to his role as the head of the family unit.

      (1) God appointed the husband to be head over the family unit (1 Corinthians 11:3). In order for the appointment to work, the wife must submit to the responsibility given to the husband by God. That is why submission by the wife to the husband constitutes an act of submission to God. O'Brien explains it this way: "God has established certain leadership and authority roles

within the family, and submission is a humble recognition of that divine ordering."[7]

(2) This type of submission is intended to restore the proper relationship of the wife to the husband established in Genesis 2:18—that of a helper to the husband, i.e., an equal and loyal partner. This relationship was messed up as a result of Adam and Eve's sin and the resulting curse on Eve: "Your desire will be for your husband, and he will rule over you" (Genesis 3:16).

(3) It is important to note that Paul did not command every woman to submit to every man. His command related only to wives with their husbands.

b. The wife is also told to submit to the husband "in everything" (5:24b). Implied in this command is an expectation that the husband is exercising his God-given responsibility in a manner that is submissive and honoring to God. Since the wife is ultimately submitted to God, her submission to her husband is limited by her responsibilities to God. Thus, if a husband is leading his family in ways that are immoral, illegal, abusive, or dangerous, the wife is not bound to submit in these areas.[8]

c. Unfortunately, this passage of Scripture has been grossly misused and abused by many husbands. Paul's command for wives to submit to their husbands does not establish a dominance of the husband over the wife, nor does it relegate the wife to a subservient role requiring her to meet her husband's every whim. In fact, Paul never tells wives to *obey* their husbands, and nowhere does Paul give husbands the right to force their wives to submit to them.[9]

2. THE HUSBAND'S RESPONSIBILITY TO SUBMIT (5:25-33)

   a. Husbands are told to fulfill their responsibility to submit to their wives, not by ruling over them, but by loving them like Christ loved the Church (5:25). While the wife is to "give in" to her husband, the husband is required to "give up" to his wife. In other words, she gives in to his leadership role, and he "gives himself up for her."

   > **Husbands fulfill their responsibility to submit to their wives by loving them like Christ loved the Church.**

   (1) The husband's headship in the family is not intended as a position of authority by which he can make demands of his wife, but instead is a position of responsibility for serving his wife in a sacrificial manner. His leadership role in the marriage is a service role, not one of lordship over the wife.

   (2) How does a husband give himself up for his wife? Paul's comparison to Christ highlighted His sacrificial love for the Church. Likewise, husbands should love their wives sacrificially, giving up their own self-interests in order to fulfill each of their wives' needs and purpose. Dwight Small, a Christian author on marriage, explains, "This may involve giving up some of their interests, their time, their pleasures, their

ambitions, and their friends. It means that nothing shall have priority over their responsibility to fulfill the needs of their wives."[10]

b. Paul compared the husband's responsibility to his wife to Christ's love for the Church. How did Christ love the Church?

(1) Christ loved the Church with a *sacrificial love* (5:25). Jesus gave up everything for the Church.[11] Likewise, a husband disobeys God when he uses his headship over the wife to get his way. Christ's headship meant sacrifice; so should the husband's.

(2) Christ loved the Church with a *sanctifying love* (5:26-27). The result of Christ's love was to make the Church holy and blameless, spiritually pure, and thus set apart to serve its proper purpose.

(a) This aspect of love requires a husband to ensure that his wife is able to fulfill her primary purpose in the marriage, that is, to be a helper to her husband. In other words, a husband must include his wife in his world by letting her in on his thoughts, feelings, dreams, and goals. To exclude her from any part of his life hinders the wife from meeting her purpose in the marriage.[12]

(b) Another aspect of the result of Christ's love for the Church mentioned in these verses is that the Church was presented to Him "as a radiant Church" (5:27). Husbands, likewise, should seek ways to honor, glorify, and exalt their wives rather than treat them with sarcasm, contempt, or rudeness. Husbands need to seek ways to make their wives feel valued, esteemed, and prized if they are going to obey God's requirement to submit to their wives by loving them.

(3) Christ loved the Church with a *caring love* (5:28-33). A husband's love for his wife should be one that shows how much he cares for her—as much care as he would show for his own body, especially since, according to Genesis 2:24 (which Paul quoted in verse 31), a husband and wife are united as one body in God's plan for marriage.

   (a) In 1 Peter 3:7, Peter described three ways husbands can show such a caring love. He said, "Husbands, in the same way be considerate as you live with your wives, and treat them with respect as the weaker partner and as heirs with you of the gracious gift of life, so that nothing will hinder your prayers."

   i. Husbands should be *considerate* of their wives. That consideration is shown through understanding, attention, and sensitivity.

   ii. Husbands should be *respectful* of their wives, treating them as "the weaker partner." Being respectful includes showing them courtesy and politeness.

   iii. Husbands should be *honoring* of their wives, treating them as co-heirs of God's gift of eternal life. Christian husbands and wives are members of an eternal family. When a husband is dishonoring to his wife, even his own spiritual life will suffer by the hindering of his prayers.[13]

(b) The one-ness of a husband and wife—and of the Church and Christ—is one of the great mysteries of Scripture (5:32).

C. *Submitting in the Family* (Ephesians 6:1-4)

1. THE CHILD'S RESPONSIBILITY TO SUBMIT (6:1-3). The child's duty to submit is performed by being obedient to his parents.

   a. The Greek word for "obey" (*hupakouete*) is a military term that means "to stand under," i.e., to do as told. Clearly, this command refers to a child who is still under his parents' authority (6:1). But in the following verse, Paul quoted the Old Testament command to "honor" our parents (Exodus 20:12, Deuteronomy 5:16), a responsibility that extends beyond childhood (6:2).

   b. This command is to be performed "in the Lord" (6:1) or for Jesus' sake and because of the child's submission to Jesus. The reason for doing so is also very simple: it is "right" (6:1b) and it "pleases the Lord" (Colossians 3:20). The Bible identifies disobedience to parents as a characteristic of wickedness (Romans 1:30) and a sign of the last days (2 Timothy 3:2).

   c. The basis for Paul's exhortation comes from the fifth of the Ten Commandments in Exodus 20:12 regarding honoring our fathers and mothers. It is the first of the commandments dealing with man's interpersonal relationships with others. The commandment includes a promise of long life, which refers to the soundness of following godly instruction from our parents (6:2-3). To the Jews in the Old Testament, the Old Testament promise referred to the community's long life in the Promised Land rather than individual promises of long earthly lives.

(1) Exodus 20:12 says, "Honor your father and your mother, so that you may live long in the land the Lord your God is giving you." The command is repeated in Deuteronomy 5:16, which says, "Honor your father and your mother, as the Lord your God has commanded you, so that you may live long and that it may go well with you in the land the Lord your God is giving you." These promises of longevity were applicable to the Israelite society, and they remain applicable to us on a societal level as well.

(2) Does the command to honor our parents only apply to us in our childhood? No. The commandment to honor our parents means more than simply obeying them as children. Its meaning continues to apply to us as adults.

   (a) The commandment means we should *treat our parents with honor and respect* throughout their lives.

      i. Solomon provided an example of this in 1 Kings 2:19 when he showed respect to his mother, Bathsheba, by standing and bowing before her and giving her a throne where she could sit at his right hand.

ii. This can be a difficult command to obey when one or both parents is or was less than honorable or respectable. But the commandment is not restricted only to worthy parents. We must still be respectful in the way we disagree with them and by forgiving them in our own hearts.[14]

(b) The commandment means we should *listen to our parents*. Proverbs 23:22 says, "Listen to your father, who gave you life, and do not despise your mother when she is old." This includes not only listening to their wisdom and advice, but also listening to their needs, especially as they age.

(c) The commandment means we should *assist our parents financially and by other practical means* as Paul explained in 1 Timothy 5:4 and 8: "If a widow has children or grandchildren, these should learn first of all to put their religion into practice by caring for their own family and so repaying their parents and grandparents, for this is pleasing to God. ... Anyone who does not provide for their relatives, and especially for their own household, has denied the faith and is worse than an unbeliever." Joseph, David, and Jesus provided examples of this aspect of the commandment in their own lives.

Ephesians 5:21-6:9

i. Joseph cared for his whole family when they arrived in Egypt. "So Joseph settled his father and his brothers in Egypt and gave them property in the best part of the land, the district of Rameses, as Pharaoh directed. Joseph also provided his father and his brothers and all his father's household with food, according to the number of their children" (Genesis 47:11-12).

ii. When David was on the run for his life from King Saul, he still found time to provide protection for his parents. "From there David went to Mizpah in Moab and said to the king of Moab, 'Would you let my father and mother come and stay with you until I learn what God will do for me?' So he left them with the king of Moab, and they stayed with him as long as David was in the stronghold" (1 Samuel 22:3-4).

iii. Jesus made sure his mother was cared for even as He hung on the cross. "Near the cross of Jesus stood his mother, his mother's sister, Mary the wife of Clopas, and Mary Magdalene. When Jesus saw his mother there, and the disciple whom he loved standing nearby, he said to her, 'Woman, here is your son,' and to the disciple, 'Here is your mother.' From that time on, this disciple took her into his home" (John 19:25-27).

iv. Authors Bill and Kathy Peel explain the importance of honoring our parents by caring for them. Referring to Christ's comments in Matthew 15:4-6 when He confronted the Pharisees about their selfish failure to care for their parents, the Peels conclude that caring for our parents in their old age is more important to God than giving Him our gifts. To care for our elderly parents is not only an act of love for them, but an act of love for God.[15]

2. THE PARENT'S RESPONSIBILITY TO SUBMIT (6:4). A parent's role in submitting is to discipline and instruct his or her children without exasperating or frustrating them with unfair and unreasonable treatment.[16]

   a. Parents are to provide their children godly discipline and instruction without exasperating or provoking them to anger.

      (1) The word for "exasperation" (*parorgitsete*) refers to the type of treatment of a child that ultimately creates within the child a resentment and hostility toward the parent.

      (2) How do parents exasperate their children? Parents can exasperate their children in several ways: overprotection, favoritism, pressuring them to achieve or expecting too much from them, discouragement, making them feel unwanted, not letting them be children, using love as a tool for reward or punishment, nagging, unfairness, physical and emotional abuse, etc.

b. One surprising way that parents may exasperate their children is by idolizing them to the point of thinking they can do no wrong. Such parents rarely discipline their children but run to their defense even when the children are wrong. As a result, those children never learn to respect others or to submit to authority, including the authority of God. We must remember that being a parent is part of our life in Christ, not the goal of our life. Consequently, Christian parents have a responsibility to teach their children to follow the commands of God. Such teaching occurs not only through verbal lessons, but also through discipline and example. The family is an important environment where we live out our position in Christ and practice true discipleship.[17]

D. *Submitting in the Workplace* (Ephesians 6:5-9)

1. THE SERVANT'S/EMPLOYEE'S RESPONSIBILITY TO SUBMIT (6:5-8). This passage is obviously inapplicable today with respect to slaves and slaveholders, but its admonitions can be extended to the employee-employer relationship. An employee's responsibility to submit is practiced by obedience to his boss with the proper attitude (6:5). As employees, we submit to our employers in the following ways:

   a. *Deferring to Our Boss's Authority.* Obedience means exactly what it sounds like: do what the boss says to do.

   b. *Respecting Our Boss's Authority.*

   (1) The attitude with which we submit to our boss is also important. An employee should obey his

or her employer "with respect and fear" (6:5a), i.e., honorably and respectfully.

(2) In addition, an employee's submission should be performed "with sincerity of heart" (6:5b). It is not a hypocritical submission, performed while we grumble under our breaths, but a genuine submission. As Christian employees, we must learn to do our work without complaining, criticizing, or being disruptive.

c. *Honoring God by Our Job Performance.*

(1) A Christian employee's motive for doing a good job should be to please and glorify Christ, not merely to "win [the bosses'] favor when their eye is on you" (6:5c).

(2) A Christian employee should not just do his job to its minimum required level. He should work hard and diligently as though he is working for God, knowing that his true rewards will come from God (6:7-8).

2. THE MASTER'S/EMPLOYER'S RESPONSIBILITY TO SUBMIT (6:9). An employer's role in submitting is to treat his employees in accordance with the will of God. He must treat them fairly and honestly. He must lead them with respect and not by threats because they are as much a child of God's as the employer is and God will not show favoritism for the employer over the employee.

Questions for Personal Reflection or Group Discussion

1. *Eph. 5:21:* What does it mean to submit to another person? Why does Paul tell us to "submit to one another"?
2. *Eph. 5:22-24:* What does it mean for a wife to submit to her husband? What is the standard by which such submission is compared?
3. *Eph. 5:25:* How does a husband submit to his wife?
4. *Eph. 5:26-28:* What are the characteristics of love that a husband should have for his wife?
5. *Eph. 6:1-3:* How do children show submission to their parents? How do adult children submit to their parents?
6. *Eph. 6:4:* How do parents "exasperate" their children?
7. *Eph. 6:5-8:* How are employees to submit to their employers?
8. *Eph. 6:9:* How are employers to submit to their employees? Why did Paul emphasize to employers (masters) that God does not show favoritism?

Chapter XI

Living With Strength and Courage
Ephesians 6:10-20

A. *Understanding the Battles We Face* **(Ephesians 6:10-13)**

1. In chapters 1-3, Paul described the assets and riches given to us by God. He reminded us of our position in Christ as believers and prayed for us to have the power to live in that position. In chapter 4, he turned to a practical discussion about how to apply the doctrines of chapters 1-3. In chapters 4-5, Paul described the kind of "walk" or life we should have as Christians: a life worthy of our calling—in unity and maturity; a life different from the world—in purity; a life as children of the light reflected by our love and wisdom; and a life of submission to one another, yielding to the needs of others around us and modeling this submissiveness in our families and workplaces.

2. Now, in chapter 6, Paul closed his letter to the Ephesians with a warning to prepare for battle.[1] The life Paul described in chapters 4-6 is not an easy one and will involve struggle to succeed. It is a difficult, unnatural, and perilous walk, fraught with the opposition of spiritual forces trying to sabotage us at every step.[2]

    a. In order to be prepared, Paul urged us to find our strength and power "in the Lord and in his mighty power" (6:10) rather than relying on our own strength or on others. In the Old Testament, virtually every follower of God's was defeated at some point or points in his life by Satan—each time when he was trying to act by his own wits or strength. This is a good reminder that we are helpless to outwit Satan by our own human power.

b. Preparation for the battle requires us to put on the "full armor of God" (6:11).

(1) Paul identified the enemy in Ephesians 6:11-12 as "the devil's schemes," referring to spiritual forces.[3]

(a) The word "schemes" is particularly appropriate for describing the methods of Satan. It reminds us that his temptations generally appear attractive and sensible at first. In fact, evil seldom appears as evil until after it has finished what it set out to do in our lives.[4]

(b) When Christians spend time and energy fighting with other people, they generally end up losing the battle because they are not fighting the real enemy. People are usually only the instrument of the evil forces of sin and Satan, but Satan's tactic is to prevent us from focusing on the real enemy. When we fight other people in a spiritual battle, we typically generate hatred and bitterness from those people because of the manner in which we fight. When we focus our efforts against the spiritual forces, however, we tend to deal with people in a more loving and compassionate manner, seeking to lead them to the Truth rather than trying to defeat them.

(2) One commentator suggests four reasons why Christians fail to be prepared for battle against spiritual forces:[5]

   (a) We do not see or believe the danger or recognize the power of the enemy.

   (b) We do not have all the weapons we need or understand the importance and significance of the weapons we have.

   (c) We are untrained in using the weapons.

   (d) We are living in a comfort zone, oblivious to the ongoing battle around us, because either we are not engaged in spiritual activities that put us in the battle or we have already compromised our lives to the enemy.

(3) Our goal in battle is not to win the victory (since Christ has already won) but to stand our ground and not give up our position as a Christian (6:13). Many Christians, however, disobey or ignore this goal or command. They do not take their salvation seriously enough to actually "take a stand," much less "stand [their] ground."

> **What does it mean for us to "stand our ground" and "to stand" on the final day?**

B. *Preparing for the Battles We Face* (Ephesians 6:14-20). In order to ensure we do not underestimate the difficulty of the battle we face, Paul reiterated for the third time our need to "stand firm" (6:14a; see also 6:11, 6:13) and then described the spiritual armor we must use in order to do so.[6] The pieces consist of two different kinds of armor: what we must "put on" (6:14-15) and what we must "take up" (6:16-17).

1. THE ARMOR WE MUST "PUT ON" (6:14-15). The first part of the armor consists of those pieces described in Ephesians 6:14-15. These are pieces that have been put on us once we became Christians, i.e., the spiritual provisions we already have. They are always on us; we simply have to realize we have them in our spiritual wardrobe and put them on in preparation for battle.

   a. *The Belt of Truth* (6:14a)

      (1) The first place we must start when we are in battle with the enemy is to be girded with the Truth.[7] The literal language says, "having girded your loins with truth" (NASB). Other versions speak of the belt being "buckled around your waist" (NIV) or the belt of truth being "fastened" (ESV). The idea of "girding one's loins" means to tuck the tunic into the belt so it would not hinder the soldier in his fight.

      (2) To do spiritual battle, we must be girded with Truth. We must understand who we are, whose we are, what we have, and where we are going. All of those things reside in our relationship with Jesus, who is the Truth and on whom we can always rely.[8] We will win these battles only when we know and are strengthened by God's Truth (which happens when we are reading and

dwelling in His Word) and when we are resolved to live by that Truth.

b. *The Breastplate of Righteousness* (6:14b)

(1) The soldier's breastplate protected his vital organs, particularly his heart. Similarly, the spiritual breastplate protects our hearts, which represent our emotional well-being.[9] When we are under attack, in addition to being grounded in the Truth, we must remember that we have been made righteous before God because of what Jesus did for us.[10] We do not stand on our own merits, but on Christ's. We are not in a position from which Christ will deliver us, but one from which Christ *has already* delivered us.

(2) Further, this piece of armor suggests we must supplement the Truth with a lifestyle that reflects the Truth and the righteousness we received. If our lifestyle is not righteous and we fail to do the right things, then we are left spiritually exposed and unprotected. As Ironside explains, "If you want to win in this battle, you must practice righteousness. Your life must be clean, there must not be hidden sin, or unholy thinking tolerated, no unrighteousness in your life covered up, if you would have victory in this conflict."[11]

c. *The Shoes of Readiness* (6:15)

(1) The soldier's shoes were hobnailed sandals that provided traction and firm footing, which were essential for standing strong in the middle of battle. As Christians, we must always be ready and prepared to stand firm in our beliefs and to

provide a ready defense. As the Apostle Peter said, "Always be prepared to give an answer to everyone who asks you to give the reason for the hope that you have" (1 Peter 3:15). Such readiness comes from knowing the "gospel of peace," i.e., the message of unity and reconciliation between us and other believers and between us and God.[12]

(2) This concept of readiness should not be understood as referring only to evangelistic activities. Readiness means having a knowledge and understanding of God's Word so that we can apply His Word to all aspects of our lives. It means living our lives consistently with God's Word so that we are able and ready to share it with others not only verbally but also through our actions by replicating the peace and love of God.

2. THE ARMOR WE MUST "TAKE UP" (6:16-17). The second part of the armor is described in Ephesians 6:16-17. These are the pieces that must be "taken up" by the Christian in the moment of battle.

   a. *The Shield of Faith* (6:16)

   (1) Paul commanded us to "take up the shield of faith" so that we can protect ourselves from the "flaming arrows of the evil one" (6:16). What kinds of arrows does Satan shoot? Satan's attacks usually come in the forms of temptation, depression, guilt, doubt, despair, false teaching, persecution, etc.

   (2) As Christians, we can ward off these arrows with faith—the assurance of God's work and

power within us and His faithfulness to keep His promises.

  (a) This is not a reference to the popular secular claim that we can overcome all obstacles by believing in ourselves. Instead, the faith Paul referred to is a faith focused on God.

  (b) The object of our faith is the important aspect of this piece of armor. Having faith in ourselves or in some esoteric philosophical concept will not help us deflect Satan's attacks. Our faith must be in God for the shield to work.

  (3) Despite their access to the shield of faith, Christians often fight their battles against "the evil one" with the wrong weapons. They trust their own moral strength and ethical ideals to always do right. But, while we need to have strong morals and ethics, these things sometimes wear down in the face of the persistent assault of evil against us. Only the resources of Christ will overcome sin, and those resources can only be appropriated by our faith in Christ.[13]

b. *The Helmet of Salvation* (6:17a). As the breastplate protects our emotional well-being, the helmet, which covers the head, protects our intellect. The truth of our salvation—not just the moment of our acceptance of Christ, but more specifically in this Scripture passage the future certainty of our salvation—will help us maintain the proper mindset in the midst of confusions and doubts.[14]

c. *The Sword of the Spirit* (6:17b). The only offensive weapon in this list is the Word of God. The Greek word translated "word" in verse 17 is not *logos*, but *rhema*. Unlike *logos*, the word *rhema* does not refer to the Bible in its entirety, "but to the individual scripture which the Spirit brings to our remembrance for use in time of need, a prerequisite being the regular storing of the mind with Scripture."[15] It emphasizes the spoken or proclaimed word of God, the word of God that comes to us in order to encourage, challenge, condemn, or speak to others as God moves us to do so.[16] Jesus' use of Scripture when being tempted in the wilderness is a good example of the use of this piece of spiritual armor (Matthew 4:1-11, Luke 4:1-13).

3. THE PRAYERS WE MUST "ALWAYS" PRAY (6:18-20). The last part of preparation for battle is prayer. Prayer is the energy source for fighting and the means for staying "alert" and ready for battle (6:18).

   a. Paul commanded us to pray "in the Spirit" (6:18a). In other words, the Holy Spirit should be intimately involved in our prayers, inspiring and guiding our prayers so that they will be effective. It is this type of prayer that distinguishes the believer's prayers from the prayers expressed by others in the world.

   b. In giving this instruction, Paul used the word "all" four times—"pray at *all* times, with *all* prayer and supplication, with *all* perseverance, and ... for *all* the saints"[17]—which provides insight into what it means to pray in the Spirit:

      (1) *When We Should Pray.* We are to pray "on all occasions" (6:18a) or at all times. We do that by maintaining a prayerful attitude throughout the day. We can voice quiet, brief prayers in the sit-

uations that we face each day. We can express gratitude to God in each circumstance that arises. As one commentator says, "You don't have to isolate yourself from other people and from daily work in order to pray constantly."[18]

(2) *How We Should Pray.*

    (a) Paul said to pray "with all kinds of prayers and requests" (6:18a). Every form of prayer

Paul's Instructions for Praying (6:18-20)	
When to Pray	On all occasions. At all times.
How to Pray	With all kinds of prayers
	With earnestness and persistence
For Whom to Pray	For all the Lord's people

is appropriate: public and private, planned and spontaneous, for self and others, prayers of praise and prayers for help, etc.

    (b) In addition, Paul encouraged us to "be alert and always keep on praying" (6:18b). He referred to earnest and persistent praying. We should always pray with the same earnestness and persistence as we do when a problem arises.

(3) *For Whom We Should Pray.* Finally, Paul said we should pray "for all the Lord's people" (6:18c). Our earnest, persistent prayers should include

prayers for other people—prayers that they would overcome the enemy and have spiritual victory. Paul provided an example of this kind of prayer when he requested prayers on his own behalf, asking them to pray that God would give him the correct words to clearly proclaim the gospel with boldness (6:19-20).

Questions for Personal Reflection or Group Discussion

1. *Eph. 6:10-12:* Against whom are we in a spiritual battle? How does it change our tactics in spiritual battle when we realize that our enemy is "not against flesh and blood"?
2. *Eph. 6:13:* What does it mean for us to "stand our ground" and "to stand" on the final day?
3. *Eph. 6:13, 16:* What is the difference between the parts of the armor of God that we must "put on" and those we must "take up"?
4. *Eph. 6:14-17:* What does each piece of the armor of God represent in our ability to fight the spiritual battles we face?
    a. Belt of truth
    b. Breastplate of righteousness
    c. Shoes of readiness
    d. Shield of faith
    e. Helmet of salvation
    f. Sword of the Spirit
5. *Eph. 6:18:* How does Paul tell us to pray? When should we pray? What kinds of prayers should we pray? For whom should we pray?
6. *Eph. 6:19-20:* Paul asked the Ephesians to pray for him in a very specific manner. Is the prayer he asked for himself a prayer we could offer for our own pastors and teachers today?

Chapter XII

Closing Statements
Ephesians 6:21-24

A. *A Commendation of Tychicus* **(Ephesians 6:21-22)**

1. Paul closed his letter to the Ephesians as he often did in other letters—with personal statements about individuals in the church to which he was writing or with other personal reflections. In this case, since he was not writing to any particular church, he mentioned only Tychicus, who was Paul's envoy to the churches in Asia Minor and the one who carried the letter to them.

    a. Tychicus was from the province of Asia and one of Paul's companions during Paul's third missionary journey as he travelled through Macedonia. Along with several others, Tychicus travelled ahead of Paul and waited for him in Troas (a city located on the west coast of Asia along the Aegean Sea) (Acts 20:3-6).

    b. Paul used Tychicus to deliver, not only this letter to the Ephesians, but also the letter to the Colossians while accompanying Onesimus, Philemon's fugitive slave (Colossians 4:7). He planned to send either Tychicus or Artemas to Crete to take Titus' place (Titus 3:12), but ended up sending Tychicus on a special mission to Ephesus during his final imprisonment shortly before Nero executed him (2 Timothy 4:12).

2. Tychicus' task was to update the recipients of the letter about how Paul was doing while he was in prison in Rome. His job was to "encourage" the recipients by letting them know that Paul was in good condition and actively preaching the gospel (6:22).

B. *A Blessing of Peace, Love, and Grace* **(Ephesians 6:23-24)**

1. Paul closed his letter with a final benediction, praying that the letter's recipients would have peace and love accompanied by faith (all of which come from God and Christ) (6:23), along with grace and the eternal love of Jesus Christ in their lives (6:24).[1]

2. These benedictions at the end of Paul's letters are often overlooked, but they provide a summary of the major themes and ideas in the letter itself.[2] In this case, Paul listed many of the incredible blessings we have from God: peace, love, faithfulness, grace, and salvation—a reminder that we have *everything we need* in order to live lives of unity, purity, enlightenment, mutual submission, and strength because He has given us "every spiritual blessing in Christ."

Questions for Personal Reflection or Group Discussion

1. *Eph. 6:21:* Consider Paul's description of Tychicus: "dear brother and faithful servant in the Lord." What does that suggest about the character of Tychicus?

2. *Eph. 6:23-24:* Paul ended his letter with a brief summary of his primary theme: that God has blessed us with "every spiritual blessing in Christ." As you end this study, consider all of the blessings Paul mentioned in this letter and what they mean to you in your daily walk with Christ.

> "Praise be to the God and Father of our Lord Jesus Christ, who has blessed us in the heavenly realms with every spiritual blessing in Christ." (1:3)

- Chosen by God (1:4)
- Adopted into God's Family (1:5)
- Given Grace (1:6)
- Redeemed, Liberated, and Forgiven (1:7)
- Informed of God's Will (1:9)
- Included in the Gospel and Appointed to be God's Witness (1:13)
- Sealed by the Holy Spirit (1:13)
- Guaranteed Redemption by the Holy Spirit (1:14)
- Hope (1:18)
- Spiritual Riches (1:18)
- Spiritual Power (1:19)
- Spiritual Life (2:4-5)
- Peace with Others through Unity and Peace with God through Reconciliation (2:13-16)
- Access to God (2:18)
- Spiritual Gifts (4:11)

Notes

INTRODUCTION

1 Peter T. O'Brien, *The Letter to the Ephesians,* The Pillar New Testament Commentary (Grand Rapids, MI: William B. Eerdmans Publishing Co., 1999), 1; Klyne Snodgrass, *Ephesians,* The NIV Application Commentary (Grand Rapids, MI: Zondervan Publishing House, 1996), 17.

2 O'Brien, *Ephesians,* 1; Snodgrass, 17.

3 John MacArthur, *Ephesians,* The MacArthur New Testament Commentary (Chicago, IL: Moody Press, 1986), vii.

4 Hetty Green was nicknamed the "Witch of Wall Street," not necessarily due to any unkindness on her part but because, after the death of her husband, she wore black mourning clothes and a heavy black veil everywhere she went. Boyden Sparkes & Samuel Taylor Moore, *The Witch of Wall Street: Hetty Green* (Garden City, KS: Garden City Publishing, 1936), 265.

5 "Hetty Green, The Richest Woman in America," *The San Francisco Call* (Mar. 26, 1899), 18, online at https://chroniclingamerica.loc.gov/lccn/sn85066387/1899-03-26/ed-1/seq-18.

6 Therese Oneill, "The Life and Times of Hetty the Hoarder, the Witch of Wall Street," *Mental Floss* (Mar. 22, 2013), online at http://mentalfloss.com/article/49379/life-and-times-hetty-hoarder-witch-wall-street.

CHAPTER I
INTRODUCTION TO THE LETTER TO THE EPHESIANS
(EPHESIANS 1:1-2)

1 O'Brien, *Ephesians*, 4; Andrew T. Lincoln, *Ephesians*, Word Biblical Commentary, vol. 42 (Dallas, TX: Word Books, 1990), lx. O'Brien claims a majority of contemporary scholars beginning in the late eighteenth and early nineteenth centuries dispute Pauline authorship of Ephesians. Generally, the scholars who do not hold to Pauline authorship do not believe the unknown writer intended to be deceptive but sought to expand upon and enhance Paul's teachings. See Stephen E. Fowl, *Ephesians: A Commentary*, The New Testament Library (Louisville, KY: Westminster John Knox Press, 2012), 10.

The primary reasons scholars have doubted Pauline authorship of Ephesians include (a) the impersonal nature of the letter and its lack of intimate connections between the author and the recipients (e.g., the nonspecific knowledge he seems to have of his readers (see, e.g., 1:13-16), his need to explain his calling as a minister to the Gentiles (3:2), and his lack of any personal greetings to members of the church); (b) the unique language and stylistic details in the letter; (c) the similarity of this letter with Colossians (34% of Colossians is paralleled in Ephesians); and (d) the different theological emphases in Ephesians than are included in other Pauline writings. O'Brien, *Ephesians*, 5-33; see also Lincoln, lx-lxxiii.

2 Early church writers attributed the authorship of Ephesians to Paul. For instance, Irenaeus, a second century theologian, expressly referred to Paul as the author of the letter. Irenaeus, *Against Heresies*, V.II.3.

With respect to the arguments against Pauline authorship, all of them can be rebutted.

(a) The impersonal nature of the letter is explained by the fact that the letter was written as a circular letter intended for several churches. It was not written specifically to the church at

Ephesus, as further explained later in this chapter's discussion of the "Recipients."

(b) While the letter to the Ephesians contains some unique literary features, they are not so unique that they bring into question Paul's authorship of the letter. For instance, Ephesians uses several distinctive terms, such as "spiritual blessing" (Ephesians 1:3) and the "devil" as a reference to Satan (Ephesians 4:27, 6:11). But, Paul often used distinctive terminology in his other letters as well in order to best explain the different issues he addressed in each letter. O'Brien, *Ephesians*, 5-6.

(c) The relationship between Ephesians and Colossians is unquestioned. But the conclusion that Ephesians so heavily borrows from Colossians as to preclude Pauline authorship of Ephesians is unsustainable. The two letters were likely written at approximately the same time, which makes their similarity unsurprising.

(d) Those who deny Paul as the author of Ephesians claim that the letter's theological emphases on Christ, salvation, the Church, and the end times are handled differently than in Paul's other letters. They believe the discussion of these doctrines reflect a different perspective than Paul's other letters. But the themes and concerns Paul addressed in the Ephesians letter likely required him to discuss these issues from a different perspective to make his point. Furthermore, in some instances, Paul's discussion of these issues may reflect a deeper and more advanced perspective on the issues than he had earlier. The change in perspective, however, is not contradictory to anything he wrote elsewhere. For a full discussion of the debate over the theological emphases in Ephesians, see O'Brien, *Ephesians*, 21-33.

3   See Bruce M. Metzger & Michael D. Coogan, eds., *The Oxford Companion to the Bible* (New York, NY: Oxford University Press, 1993), 41; Lawrence O. Richards, *Zondervan Expository Diction-*

ary of Bible Words (Grand Rapids, MI: Zondervan Publishing House, 1991), 59.

4 Metzger & Coogan, *The Oxford Companion to the Bible*, 41. See, e.g., 1 Samuel 25:9.

5 This is the same designation Paul used in 1 Corinthians 1:1, 2 Corinthians 1:1, Colossians 1:1, and 2 Timothy 1:1.

6 O'Brien, *Ephesians*, 57. Those who dispute Pauline authorship date it between 80-90 A.D. See Lincoln, lxxiii.

7 O'Brien, *Ephesians*, 87; Lincoln, 6.

8 H.A. Ironside, *Ephesians*, An Ironside Expository Commentary (Grand Rapids, MI: Kregel Publications, 2007), 11.

9 Snodgrass, 39.

10 Ibid., 38-39.

11 O'Brien, *Ephesians*, 47. Being a circular letter explains one of the reasons why it is so general in nature and does not show the intimate connection between Paul and the readers that seems to exist in Paul's other letters.

12 Maxie D. Dunnam, *Galatians, Ephesians, Philippians, Colossians, & Philemon*, The Communicator's Commentary, vol. 8 (Dallas, TX: Word Publishing, 1982), 138.

13 Ralph P. Martin, "Ephesians," *2 Corinthians-Philemon*, The Broadman Bible Commentary, vol. 11 (Nashville, TN: Broadman Press, 1971), 127.

14 Ronald Youngblood, ed., *Nelson's New Illustrated Bible Dictionary* (Nashville, TN: Thomas Nelson Publishers, 1995), 406-407.

15 It is interesting to note that all of Paul's letters begin and end with a reference to God's grace.

16 See Snodgrass, 23. Some commentators distinguish between the two letters' purposes by noting that Paul's letter to the Ephesians focused on the Church as the body of Christ, where-

as his letter to the Colossians focused on Christ as the head of the Church. Accordingly, the purpose of Ephesians was about the Church's responsibility to fulfill Christ's work.

17 O'Brien, *Ephesians*, 58.

18 Ibid., 57.

19 Snodgrass, 23.

CHAPTER II
EVERY SPIRITUAL BLESSING IN CHRIST
(EPHESIANS 1:3-14)

1 Paul used a format for his praise similar to the Jewish eulogies of the Old Testament known as a *berakah*. O'Brien, *Ephesians*, 89. A *berakah* was typically formulated with the words "Blessed be God who has ...." Some Old Testament examples of a *berakah* are found in Solomon's prayer in 1 Kings 8:15 and 56 and at the end of each book of the Psalms in Psalms 41:13; 72:18-19; 89:52; and 106:48. See Lincoln, 10.

2 MacArthur, 8.

3 O'Brien, *Ephesians*, 97.

4 Snodgrass, 21, 47. William Klein refers to this as "realized eschatology." William W. Klein, "Ephesians," *Ephesians-Philemon*, The Expositor's Bible Commentary rev. ed., vol. 12, Tremper Longman III & David E. Garland, eds. (Grand Rapids, MI: Zondervan, 2006), 48.

5 References to believers being "in Christ" appear ten times in this single passage (i.e., Ephesians 1:3-14).

6 See, e.g., John 1:12; Romans 10:9, 13.

7 Klein, 49; Ironside, 21.

8 Snodgrass, 49.

9 Charles Spurgeon explained the reason he believed in the doctrine of election from a personal perspective. He said, "I believe the doctrine of election, because I am quite certain that, if God had not chosen me, I should never have chosen Him; and I am sure He chose me before I was born, or else He never would have chosen me afterwards; and He must have elected me for reasons unknown to me, for I never could find any reason in myself why He should have looked upon me with special love. So I am forced to accept that great Biblical doctrine." C.H. Spurgeon, *C.H. Spurgeon's Autobiography,* Vol. I (London, ENG: Passmore and Alabaster, 1897), 170, available online at *Internet Archive*, https://archive.org/details/spurgeonsautobio01spuruoft.

10 O'Brien, *Ephesians,* 101; Dunnam, 149.

11 There is a grammatical difficulty in verse 4 in determining whether the phrase "in love" modifies the prior clause or the succeeding clause. Commentators seem to be split, but the meaning of either translation remains biblically accurate. Either God views us as holy and blameless in love or He predestined us to adoption in love. Of course, both statements are true. See O'Brien, *Ephesians,* 101 (preferring to attach the phrase to the preceding clause); Snodgrass, 50 (preferring to attach the phrase to the succeeding clause).

12 O'Brien, *Ephesians,* 105.

13 See Romans 6:18.

14 See Hebrews 9:22; 1 Peter 1:18-19.

15 Ironside, 35.

16 Some scholars and translations (including the New International Version, English Standard Version, and New American Standard Bible) interpret the phrase "with all wisdom and understanding" as qualifying the language in the succeeding verse 9, thus making it a reference to God's wisdom and understanding for making known the mystery of His will. See

Snodgrass, 53. Others, however, link the phrase with the preceding statement in verse 8, meaning that wisdom and understanding are additional gifts God has given to us along with His abundant grace (which is the interpretation followed in these Bible Study Notes). See O'Brien, *Ephesians,* 107; Lincoln, 17, 29.18

17 Bruce B. Barton, et al., *Ephesians,* Life Application Bible Commentary (Wheaton, IL: Tyndale House Publishers, Inc., 1996), 20. See also Proverbs 9:10.

18 O'Brien, *Ephesians,* 107-109; Lincoln, 29-30.

19 O'Brien, *Ephesians,* 109. Paul referred to mysteries twenty-one times in his letters, out of twenty-seven total times in the New Testament. Ibid. The mysteries Paul described were not different mysteries but are different aspects of the same mystery regarding salvation: the future salvation of the Jews (Romans 11:25), the Rapture (1 Corinthians 15:51), the availability of salvation to Gentiles (Ephesians 3:6-9; Colossians 1:26-27), and the union of Christ and the Church (Ephesians 5:32).

20 See Philippians 2:10-11.

21 O'Brien, *Ephesians,* 115. Klein, on the other hand, argues that the "we/you" distinction is not Jew/Gentile but a reference to Christians who believed first ("we") and the Ephesian believers who believed later (you"). Klein, 53-54; see also Lincoln, 37.

22 See Romans 8:38-39.

23 Billy Graham, *The Holy Spirit: Activating God's Power in Your Life* (Waco, TX: Warner Books, 1978), 109.

24 See also 2 Corinthians 1:21-22; 2 Corinthians 5:5.

25 Matthew Henry, *Commentary on the Whole Bible,* Vol. 6, s.v. Eph. 1:14 (1706).

26 Barton, et al., 27; see also MacArthur, 36.

CHAPTER III
PAUL'S PRAYER FOR OUR ENLIGHTENMENT
(EPHESIANS 1:15-23)

1 See John 13:35; James 2:17.

2 John R.W. Stott, *The Message of Ephesians: God's New Society* (Downers Grove, IL: Inter-Varsity Press, 1979), 52.

3 See O'Brien, *Ephesians*, 130; Snodgrass, 72-73; Klein, 58.

4 See section C.1.b(3)(a) in chapter II.

5 Arthur W. Pink, *The Ability of God: Prayers of the Apostle Paul* (Chicago, IL: Moody Press, 2000), 148-149.

6 Klein, 58.

7 O'Brien, *Ephesians*, 134.

8 The word "glorious" may better be translated as modifying "riches." The Holman Christian Standard Bible translates the verse this way: "I pray that the perception of your mind may be enlightened so you may know what is the hope of His calling, what are *the glorious riches of His inheritance* among the saints" (emphasis added).

9 Barton, et al., 31.

10 Snodgrass, 78.

11 Ibid., 80; O'Brien, *Ephesians*, 149. For example, in Colossians 1:19, Paul explained that "the fullness of God was pleased to dwell" in Christ (ESV).

12 The latter statement represents O'Brien's view. He believes the verse refers to the Church as the body and fullness of Christ who fills all things. In this interpretation, Christ fills the Church, rather than the Church filling Christ. O'Brien, *Ephesians*, 152; see also Klein, 62; Lincoln, 76.

13 Dunnam, 165; David. C. George, *2 Corinthians, Galatians, Ephesians,* Layman's Bible Book Commentary, vol. 21 (Nashville, TN: Broadman Press, 1979), 105.

14 Barton, et al., 32.

CHAPTER IV
FROM DEATH TO LIFE
(EPHESIANS 2:1-10)

1 Verses 1-7 in chapter 2 constitute another single sentence in the Greek.

2 Ray Stedman, *Our Riches in Christ: Discovering the Believer's Inheritance in Ephesians* (Grand Rapids, MI: Discovery House Publishers, 1998), 75.

3 Snodgrass, 95.

4 O'Brien, *Ephesians,* 157; Lincoln, 93.

5 MacArthur, 54. See also Matthew 12:35; 15:18-19.

6 Fowl, 69; Martin, 141. Martin points out that the English word "lunacy" comes from the Latin word *luna,* which means moon.

7 William Barclay, *The Letters to the Galatians and Ephesians,* rev. ed., The Daily Bible Study Series (Louisville, KY: Westminster John Knox Press, 1979), 101.

8 Klein, 67.

9 Paul frequently used a "formerly/now" or "already/not yet" contrast throughout the letter to the Ephesians. This is the first of five in the letter. Snodgrass, 93.

10 The NIV translation, which adds the dependent clause between "but" and "God," does not reflect the fact that the emphasis in Ephesians 2:4 is on God. The ESV and NASB versions start with "But God."

11 Klein, 71.

CHAPTER V
JESUS' PEACE MISSION
(EPHESIANS 2:11-22)

1. In 1878, Randolph McCoy accused Floyd Hatfield, a cousin of William Hatfield (also known as Devil Ance, the family patriarch), of stealing a pig. But Floyd was cleared of the charges in a trial presided over by another Hatfield cousin, based largely on the testimony of a man named Bill Staton. Two years later, McCoy's nephew killed Staton.

    In 1882, three of McCoy's sons got into a fight with Hatfield's two brothers, resulting in one of the McCoys stabbing one of the Hatfields multiple times and shooting him in the back. The Hatfields caught the McCoy boys, tied them to some bushes, and fired more than fifty shots into them, killing all three of them.

    Indictments were issued against twenty of the Hatfields, but the Hatfields eluded arrest. On New Year's Day 1888, the Hatfields attacked McCoy's home, killed his son and daughter, and badly beat his wife. Ultimately, the Hatfields were caught and tried. Most were given life imprisonment, and one of them was hanged.

    The feud began to fade after this. Randolph McCoy became a ferry operator and died in 1914 at age 88. William "Devil Ance" Hatfield became a born again believer and was baptized at age 73. He died in 1921 at age 82.

    "The Hatfield & McCoy Feud," *History.com*, online at https://www.history.com/shows/hatfields-and-mccoys/articles/the-hatfield-mccoy-feud.

2. O'Brien, *Ephesians*, 183.

3. This is similar to God's exhortation to the Israelites to remember their time of slavery in Egypt (see, e.g., Deuteronomy 15:15). The purpose of remembering our past is to attain great-

er recognition and appreciation of what God did for us. O'Brien, *Ephesians*, 185.

4   The concept of "far" and "near" may have been an allusion to Isaiah 57:19.

5   Merriam-Webster.com, s.v. "Peace," online at https://www.merriam-webster.com/dictionary/peace.

6   When using this phrase, Paul may have had in mind the Temple balustrade that separated the Court of the Gentiles from the Court of Women at the Temple (although he clearly had in mind more than merely physical barriers). Warning signs, written in both Greek and Roman, hung around the balustrade of the Temple that said, "No foreigner is to go beyond the balustrade and the plaza of the temple zone. Whoever is caught doing so will have himself to blame for his death which will follow." "Archaeology and the Temple," *Bible History*, online at https://www.bible-history.com/jewishtemple/JEWISH_TEMPLEArchaeology.htm; see also Josephus, *The Wars of the Jews* 5.5(194).

7   See Snodgrass, 133. O'Brien takes a different view and believes the reference to the law is to all Old Testament law. He said, "Perhaps it may help to say that what is abolished is the 'law-covenant,' that is, the law as a whole conceived as a covenant. It is then replaced by a new covenant for Jews *and* Gentiles." O'Brien, *Ephesians*, 199.

8   Stedman defines "self-righteousness" as "the demand that the other person change without admitting your own need for change." Stedman, 157-158.

9   Merriam-Webster.com, s.v. "Reconcile," online at https://www.merriam-webster.com/dictionary/reconcile.

10 Dunnam, 175.

11 This statement includes all of the persons of the Trinity in their functional aspects: God the Son provides access to God the Fa-

Bible Study Notes on Ephesians

ther through the work of God the Holy Spirit. See also 1 Peter 3:18.

12 See also 1 Peter 2:4-6; Revelation 21:3.

13 Ironside, 83.

14 Paul described the incredible blessings and responsibilities of the Jews in Romans 9:4-5.

CHAPTER VI
PAUL'S PRAYER FOR POWER
(EPHESIANS 3:1-21)

1 See Acts 22:21-22, where Paul announced to a crowd of Jews that God called him to preach to the Gentiles. The resulting uproar from the crowd led the Roman soldiers to arrest Paul, the beginning of his long imprisonment in Caesarea and Rome.

2 Patrick Thean, "How to Connect Execution to Your Strategy," *Rhythm Systems* (May 28, 2014), online at https://www.rhythmsystems.com/blog/how-to-connect-execution-to-your-strategy; see also Barclay, 121.

3 Barclay, 122.

4 See Dunnam, 179.

5 Pauls' reference to earlier writings in verse 3 probably refers to his writings about the mystery in chapters 1 and 2, not to a separate letter or document. Ibid.

6 See O'Brien, *Ephesians*, 232.

7 Ibid., 240.

8 Paul said that his responsibility was to "make plain to everyone" (Ephesians 3:9) the mystery God revealed to him. By claiming this responsibility, Paul recognized that this enlightenment was available to all people although it may not be accepted by all. He was in no way teaching a doctrine of universal salvation. Klein, 90.

9 O'Brien, *Ephesians,* 246.

10 Warren W. Weirsbe, *Be Rich: Gaining the Things That Money Can't Buy* (Wheaton, IL: Victor Books, 1984), 74.

11 Lincoln, 190.

12 O'Brien, *Ephesians,* 250.

13 Snodgrass, 176.

14 This is a similar idea to James' teaching in James 1:22 that we not only be hearers of the word but also doers of the word.

15 Commentators talk much about Paul's position of prayer, "[kneeling] before the Father" (Ephesians 3:14). It is unlikely he intended to make any particular point from this statement other than that he humbled himself before God as he prayed for his readers. Sam Walter Foss' poem, "The Prayer of Cyrus Brown," may best explain, in a humorous way, the relative unimportance of our position in prayer:

> "The proper way for a man to pray,"
> Said Deacon Lemuel Keyes,
> "And the only proper attitude
> Is down upon his knees."
>
> "No, I should say the way to pray,"
> Said Rev. Doctor Wise,
> "Is standing straight with outstretched arms
> And rapt and upturned eyes."
>
> "Oh, no; no, no," said Elder Slow,
> "Such posture is too proud:
> A man should pray with eyes fast closed
> And head contritely bowed."
>
> "It seems to me his hands should be
> Austerely clasped in front.
> With both thumbs pointing toward the ground,"
> Said Rev. Doctor Blunt.

> "Las' year I fell in Hodgkin's well
> Head first," said Cyrus Brown,
> "With both my heels a-stickin' up,
> My head a-pinting down;
>
> An' I made a prayer right then an' there—
> Best prayer I ever said,
> The prayingest prayer I ever prayed,
> A-standin' on my head."

16 Ironside, 91-92.

17 O'Brien, *Ephesians*, 256; Klein, 97. Lincoln believes the phrase refers to angels only. Lincoln, 202.

18 MacArthur, 100. More accurately, Paul had only one main request—the empowerment of the Holy Spirit—which he explained further in the remainder of his prayer. Snodgrass, 178.

19 For other examples of Paul's prayers for the spiritual needs of others, see Philippians 1:9-10 and Colossians 1:9-11.

20 Lincoln, 207.

21 MacArthur, 106.

22 Ibid., 107.

23 The New International Version obscures the fact that the phrase "the breadth and length and height and depth" (Ephesians 3:18 ESV) has no direct object. The New International Version translation, however, constitutes the most popular interpretation among commentators, identifying the "love of Christ" as the direct object, but other ideas suggest the phrase refers to the power of God, the mystery of salvation, or the wisdom of God. O'Brien, *Ephesians*, 261-263.

24 "The apostle Paul was accustomed to asking God for extravagant blessings on behalf of his Christian readers .... Has the apostle, then, 'gone over the top'? No, for it is impossible to ask

for too much since the Father's giving exceeds their capacity for asking or even imagining." O'Brien, *Ephesians,* 266.

25 MacArthur, 113.

CHAPTER VII
LIVING IN UNITY
(EPHESIANS 4:1-16)

1   Dunnam, 195-196.

2   W.E. Vine, *An Expository Dictionary of New Testament Words,* vol. III, s.v. "Meek, Meekness" (Old Tappan, NJ: Fleming H. Revell Co., 1966), 56.

3   O'Brien, *Ephesians,* 278.

4   These unity statements comprise a Trinitarian confession using three triads: The Holy Spirit (body, Spirit, hope); Jesus Christ (Lord, faith, baptism); and God the Father (over, through, and in all). See Klein, 108-109. The final triad has its own Trinitarian aspect as well, with the Father being "over" us, the Son "through" us, and the Spirit "in" us.

5   Millard J. Erickson, *Introducing Christian Doctrine,* 2d ed. (Grand Rapids, MI: Baker Academic, 2001), 88-89.

6   Ibid., 87.

7   Wayne Grudem, *Bible Doctrine: Essential Teachings of the Christian Faith* (Grand Rapids, MI: Zondervan, 1999), 127.

8   It is interesting to note that the giving of spiritual gifts is an act of the full Godhead. In 1 Corinthians 12:11, the Spirit is identified as the one giving the gifts. In Romans 12:3, God is the giver. Here, in Ephesians 4:7, Christ is the one who apportions the gifts. See O'Brien, *Ephesians,* 287-288.

9   Derek Kidner, *Psalms 1-72,* Tyndale Old Testament Commentaries (Downers Grove, IL: Inter-Varsity Press, 1973), 238.

10 Marvin E. Tate, *Psalms 51-100,* Word Biblical Commentary (Dallas, TX: Word Books, 1990), 184.

11 Kidner, 242 n.2. Other explanations of why Paul changed the scripture quotation are discussed in O'Brien, *Ephesians,* 289-293.

12 Barclay, 144.

13 Others interpret the descent "to the lower, earthly regions" in a couple of different ways. One is that it means Christ descended into Hades during His three days in the tomb (citing 1 Peter 3:18-22), while other interpretations see it as a reference to the Holy Spirit's descent at Pentecost. O'Brien, *Ephesians,* 296.

14 There are other listings of spiritual gifts in 1 Corinthians 12:8-10, 28-30; Romans 12:6-9; and 1 Peter 4:11.

15 *The New Compact Bible Dictionary* (Grand Rapids, MI: Zondervan Publishing House, 1967), s.v. "Apostle," 48.

16 Stedman, 201-202.

17 Snodgrass, 212.

18 Ibid., 206. Lincoln, however, believes the word solely refers to "speaking the truth" and has nothing to do with actions. Lincoln, 259.

19 Ironside, 116.

CHAPTER VIII
LIVING IN PURITY
(EPHESIANS 4:17-5:2)

1 R.G. Bratcher & E.A. Nida, *A Handbook on Paul's Letter to the Ephesians,* UBS New Testament Handbook Series, s.v. Ephesians 4:17-18 (New York, NY: United Bible Societies, 1982). Paul said something similar about godless people in Romans 1:21-23.

2 O'Brien, *Ephesians,* 321.

Notes

3 F.F. Bruce, *Paul: Apostle of the Free Spirit* (Grand Rapids, MI: Paternoster Press, 1977), 355. Barclay says the Greek word for "hardening" (*porosin*) is the word for petrify and originally referred to a stone that was harder than marble. In time, it was also used to refer to the calcification that forms around a broken bone and ultimately becomes harder than the bone itself. Barclay, 152; see also MacArthur, 169.

4 O'Brien, *Ephesians*, 322.

5 Barton, et al., 90.

6 Cleon L. Rogers Jr. & Cleon L. Rogers III, *The New Linguistic and Exegetical Key to the Greek New Testament* (Grand Rapids, MI: Zondervan Publishing House, 1998), 441.

7 O'Brien, *Ephesians*, 323.

8 Ibid., 329. The command is reminiscent of Paul's admonition in Romans 12:2.

9 See Barton, et al., 93.

10 Stedman, 237.

11 Ibid., 241.

12 Paul apparently had Zechariah 8:16 in mind, which says: "These are the things you are to do: Speak the truth to each other …."

13 Glen A. Blanscet, *Lessons from Solomon: Finding True Success in Life* (Bloomington, IN: WestBow Press, 2018), 86-87.

14 Sam Harris, *Lying* (N.p.: Four Elephants Press, 2013), 28.

15 O'Brien, *Ephesians*, 340. See Jesus's teaching on reconciliation in Matthew 5:23-24.

16 Snodgrass, 251; Lincoln, 305.

17 See also Ephesians 5:4-5.

18 Blanscet, 90.

19 Martin, 161-162.

20 O'Brien, *Ephesians,* 349; Klein, 132.

21 W.E. Vine, *An Expository Dictionary of New Testament Words,* vol. I, s.v. "Anger, Angry" (Old Tappan, NJ: Fleming H. Revell Co., 1966), 55-56.

CHAPTER IX
LIVING AS CHILDREN OF LIGHT
(EPHESIANS 5:3-21)

1 Snodgrass, 268; O'Brien, *Ephesians,* 359.

2 O'Brien, *Ephesians,* 364.

3 Ibid.

4 On the other hand, if an immoral person claims to be a believer, we *are* commanded to cut off association with him or her until the person repents. See 1 Corinthians 5:9-11.

5 The source of the quotation in verse 14 is unknown. It does not correspond to any Old Testament Scripture, so it is possible it was a common hymn sung in Paul's day.

6 Verses 18-21 are one sentence in the original Greek. Thus, while verse 21 is an appropriate heading for the subsequent instructions Paul provided for the family and workplace, it is also part of Paul's description of the results of being filled with the Holy Spirit. See O'Brien, *Ephesians,* 386-388.

7 See MacArthur, 247-248.

8 See, e.g., John 3:34b: "God gives the Spirit without limit."

9 These illustrations are adapted from MacArthur, 250.

10 O'Brien argues that the meaning of submission in Ephesians 5:21 is not a mutual submission among believers but a submission to those in authority over them, which as Paul explained in the subsequent verses consists of wives submitting to their

husbands, children to their fathers, and servants to their masters. O'Brien, *Ephesians,* 400-405. But the context of the statement suggests that Paul was speaking of a mutual submission because, in the same passage, he described the responsibility of husbands to submit to their wives, fathers to their children, and masters to their servants. Paul described submission, therefore, in a mutual manner.

11 Ironside, 152.

CHAPTER X
LIVING IN MUTUAL SUBMISSION
(EPHESIANS 5:21-6:9)

1 The longest section in this passage on relationships addresses the husband-wife relationship, taking up twelve verses with forty words about wives and one hundred fifteen words about husbands. The other sections include four verses relating to the parent-child relationship and five verses to the master-slave relationship. O'Brien, *Ephesians,* 409.

2 See Dunnam, 230-231.

3 Stedman, 304.

4 For a thorough discussion of the background of house codes, see Peter T. O'Brien, *Colossians, Philemon,* Word Biblical Commentary, vol. 44 (Waco, TX: Word Books, 1982), 214-219.

5 Stedman, 307.

6 In the original Greek, there is no actual verb in verse 22. Thus, Ephesians 5:22 actually says, "Wives, to your own husbands, as to the Lord." The verb used in this verse is borrowed from verse 21. Snodgrass, 287.

7 O'Brien, *Ephesians,* 411.

8 The limit on submitting to authorities when they act in opposition to God's will is illustrated elsewhere in Scripture. For example, when the Sanhedrin ordered Peter to stop preaching

about Jesus Christ, Peter replied, "We must obey God rather than human beings" (Acts 5:29).

9   Snodgrass, 294.

10 Dwight Small, "The Lover," *The Marriage Affair*, J. Allan Peterson, ed. (Wheaton, IL: Tyndale House Publishers, 1971), 85.

11 See Philippians 2:5-8.

12 Stedman, 316.

13 MacArthur, 304.

14 Bill Peel & Kathy Peel, *Where is Moses When We Need Him: Teaching Your Kids the Ten Values that Matter Most* (Nashville, TN: Broadman & Holman Publishers, 1995), 135.

15 Ibid., 138.

16 The Greek word, *pateres*, can also be translated "parents," but it appears Paul's focus was on fathers in particular. Snodgrass, 322.

17 Snodgrass, 330.

CHAPTER XI
LIVING WITH STRENGTH AND COURAGE
(EPHESIANS 6:10-20)

1   In technical terms, rhetoricians refer to this section as a *peroratio*, a closing section of a speech that attempts to recap what has been said earlier and arouse the listeners or readers to action. See Snodgrass, 335.

2   Snodgrass points out that the commands in this section are plural, highlighting the fact that Paul's instructions were primarily intended for the Church rather than individuals. This is not to deny their relevance to individuals, but it is important to remember it is specifically the Church that is called to "be strong," "put on the full armor of God," and "stand." Ibid., 339; see also Klein, 162.

3   "Christ's triumph over the powers has 'already' occurred (1:21), so believers no longer live in fear of them. But the fruits of that victory have 'not yet' been fully realized, so Christians must be aware of the conflict and be equipped with divine power to stand against them." O'Brien, *Ephesians,* 458-459.

4   Snodgrass, 339.

5   Barton, et al., 129.

6   Throughout the entire epistle, Paul utilized a spiritual progression based on the verbs "sit," "walk," and "stand." In the first part of the letter, he emphasized our possessions and position in Christ, summarized best by his statement that God "*seated* us with him in the heavenly realms in Christ Jesus" (Ephesians 2:6, emphasis added). In the second part of the letter, Paul repeatedly urged his readers to "*walk* in a manner worthy of the calling to which you have been called" (Ephesians 4:1 ESV, emphasis added). In the last part of the letter, Paul concluded with the exhortation to "*stand* firm" (Ephesians 6:14, emphasis added) so that we maintain and utilize the blessings and position we already received. See Lincoln, 460.

7   Paul's reference to a "belt of truth" may be an allusion to Isaiah 11:5.

8   See Hebrews 13:8.

9   Paul may have taken the idea of the "breastplate of righteousness" from Isaiah 59:17. Klein warns against allegorizing the individual pieces of armor or exploiting the symbolism they bear. Instead, he encourages seeking Paul's true intent in the metaphor. Klein, 168.

10 See Romans 8:1.

11 Ironside, 182.

12 Paul's reference to shoes of readiness is probably taken from Isaiah 52:7. Lincoln highlights the paradox of Paul's illustration

by noting that we are prepared for war only when we take up the gospel of peace. Lincoln, 449.

13 Dunnam, 242-243.

14 See also 1 Thessalonians 5:8.

15 W.E. Vine, *An Expository Dictionary of New Testament Words*, vol. IV (Old Tappan, NJ: Fleming H. Revell Co., 1966), 230.

16 O'Brien, *Ephesians*, 482; Dunnam, 244.

17 O'Brien, *Ephesians*, 483.

18 Barton, et al., 136.

CHAPTER XII
CLOSING STATEMENTS
(EPHESIANS 6:21-24)

1 The final clause "with an undying love" is unclear as to its meaning. The Greek word, *aphtharsia*, means immortality or incorruptibility. The alternative reading in the New International Version footnote provides perhaps the best understanding of the phrase: "Grace and immortality to all who love our Lord Jesus Christ" (Ephesians 6:24 note b). See O'Brien, *Ephesians*, 494-495; Lincoln, 467-468. On the other hand, Snodgrass prefers to interpret the phrase as relating to Jesus Christ, in which case it emphasizes the fact that He already reigns in immortality. Snodgrass, 365.

2 See Jeffrey A.D. Weima, "The Pauline Letter Closings: Analysis and Hermeneutical Significance," *Bulletin for Biblical Research* 5:177-198 (1995).

Sources Cited

"Archaeology and the Temple." *Bible History.* Online at https://www.bible-history.com/jewishtemple/JEWISH_TEM PLEArchaeology.htm.

Barclay, William. *The Letters to the Galatians and Ephesians,* rev. ed. The Daily Bible Study Series. Louisville, KY: Westminster John Knox Press. 1979.

Barton, Bruce B. et al. *Ephesians.* Life Application Bible Commentary. Wheaton, IL: Tyndale House Publishers, Inc. 1996.

Blanscet, Glen A. *Lessons from Solomon: Finding True Success in Life.* Bloomington, IN: WestBow Press. 2018.

Bratcher, R.G. & E.A. Nida. *A Handbook on Paul's Letter to the Ephesians.* UBS New Testament Handbook Series. New York, NY: United Bible Societies. 1982.

Bruce, F.F. *Paul: Apostle of the Free Spirit.* Grand Rapids, MI: Paternoster Press. 1977.

Dunnam, Maxie D. *Galatians, Ephesians, Philippians, Colossians, & Philemon.* The Communicator's Commentary. Vol. 8. Dallas, TX: Word Publishing. 1982.

Erickson, Millard J. *Introducing Christian Doctrine.* 2d ed. Grand Rapids, MI: Baker Academic. 2001.

Foss, Sam Walter. "The Prayer of Cyrus Brown."

Fowl, Stephen E. *Ephesians: A Commentary.* The New Testament Library. Louisville, KY: Westminster John Knox Press. 2012.

George, David C. *2 Corinthians, Galatians, Ephesians.* Layman's Bible Book Commentary. Vol. 21. Nashville, TN: Broadman Press. 1979.

Graham, Billy. *The Holy Spirit: Activating God's Power in Your Life.* Waco, TX: Warner Books. 1978.

Grudem, Wayne. *Bible Doctrine: Essential Teachings of the Christian Faith.* Grand Rapids, MI: Zondervan. 1999.

Harris, Sam. *Lying.* N.p.: Four Elephants Press. 2013.

"The Hatfield & McCoy Feud." History.com. Online at https://www.history.com/shows/hatfields-and-mccoys/articles/the-hatfield-mccoy-feud.

Henry, Matthew. *Commentary on the Whole Bible.* 1706.

"Hetty Green, The Richest Woman in America." *The San Francisco Call.* Mar. 26, 1899. Online at https://chroniclingamerica.loc.gov/lccn/sn85066387/1899-03-26/ed-1/seq-18.

Irenaeus. *Against Heresies.*

Ironside, H.A. *Ephesians.* An Ironside Expository Commentary. 1920. Grand Rapids, MI: Kregel Publications. 2007.

Josephus. *The Wars of the Jews.*

Kidner, Derek. *Psalms 1-72.* Tyndale Old Testament Commentaries. Downers Grove, IL: Inter-Varsity Press. 1973.

Klein, William W. "Ephesians." *Ephesians-Philemon.* The Expositor's Bible Commentary, rev. ed. Vol. 12. Tremper Longman III & David E. Garland, eds. Grand Rapids, MI: Zondervan. 2006.

Lincoln, Andrew T. *Ephesians*. Word Biblical Commentary. Vol. 42. Dallas, TX: Word Books. 1990.

MacArthur, John. *Ephesians*. The MacArthur New Testament Commentary. Chicago, IL: Moody Press. 1986.

Martin, Ralph P. "Ephesians." *2 Corinthians-Philemon*. The Broadman Bible Commentary. Vol. 11. Nashville, TN: Broadman Press. 1971.

Merriam-Webster.com. Online at https://www.merriam-webster.com.

Metzger, Bruce M. & Michael D. Coogan, eds. *The Oxford Companion to the Bible*. New York, NY: Oxford University Press. 1993.

The New Compact Bible Dictionary. Grand Rapids, MI: Zondervan Publishing House. 1967.

O'Brien, Peter T. *Colossians, Philemon*. Word Biblical Commentary. Vol. 44. Waco, TX: Word Books. 1982.

_____. *The Letter to the Ephesians*. The Pillar New Testament Commentary. Grand Rapids, MI: William B. Eerdmans Publishing Co. 1999.

Oneill, Therese. "The Life and Times of Hetty the Hoarder, the Witch of Wall Street." *Mental Floss*. Mar. 22, 2013. Online at http://mentalfloss.com/article/49379/life-and-times-hetty-hoarder-witch-wall-street.

Peel, Bill & Kathy Peel. *Where is Moses When We Need Him: Teaching Your Kids the Ten Values that Matter Most*. Nashville, TN: Broadman & Holman Publishers. 1995.

Pink, Arthur W. *The Ability of God: Prayers of the Apostle Paul*. Chicago, IL: Moody Press. 2000.

Richards, Lawrence O. *Zondervan Expository Dictionary of Bible Words*. Grand Rapids, MI: Zondervan Publishing House. 1991.

Rogers Jr., Cleon L. & Cleon L. Rogers III. *The New Linguistic and Exegetical Key to the Greek New Testament*. Grand Rapids, MI: Zondervan Publishing House. 1998.

Small, Dwight. "The Lover." *The Marriage Affair*. J. Allan Peterson, ed. Wheaton, IL: Tyndale Hose Publishers. 1971.

Snodgrass, Klyne. *Ephesians*. The NIV Application Commentary. Grand Rapids, MI: Zondervan Publishing House. 1996.

Sparkes, Boyden & Samuel Taylor Moore. *The Witch of Wall Street: Hetty Green*. Garden City, KS: Garden City Publishing. 1936.

Spurgeon, C.H. *C.H. Spurgeon's Autobiography*. Vol. I. London, ENG: Passmore and Alabaster. 1897. Online at *Internet Archive*, https://archive.org/details/spurgeonsautobio01spuruoft.

Stedman, Ray. *Our Riches in Christ: Discovering the Believer's Inheritance in Ephesians*. Grand Rapids, MI: Discovery House Publishers. 1998.

Stott, John R.W. *The Message of Ephesians: God's New Society*. Downers Grove, IL: Inter-Varsity Press. 1979.

Tate, Marvin E. *Psalms 51-100*. Word Biblical Commentary. Dallas, TX: Word Books. 1990.

Thean, Patrick. "How to Connect Execution to Your Strategy." *Rhythm Systems*. May 28, 2014. Online at https://www.rhythmsystems.com/blog/how-to-connect-execution-to-your-strategy.

Vine, W.E. *An Expository Dictionary of New Testament Words.* Old Tappan, NJ: Fleming H. Revell Co. 1966.

Weima, Jeffrey A.D. "The Pauline Letter Closings: Analysis and Hermeneutical Significance." *Bulletin for Biblical Research* 5:177-198. 1995.

Weirsbe, Warren W. *Be Rich: Gaining the Things That Money Can't Buy.* Wheaton, IL: Victor Books., 1984.

Youngblood, Ronald, ed. *Nelson's New Illustrated Bible Dictionary.* Nashville, TN: Thomas Nelson Publishers. 1995.

Also by the Author

Lessons from Solomon: Finding True Success in Life provides an engaging and thought-provoking look at the life of King Solomon in the Bible and draws specific lessons from his vast life experiences—both the successes and the failures—that we can apply in our own personal quests to find true success in life.

The book is available in hardcover, softcover, and eBook formats wherever books are sold online. The book is also available on the author's website at www.glenblanscet.com.

"Based on the life of Solomon, Blanscet has distilled from Solomon's story the life lessons that lead us to genuine success from the wisest man who ever lived. I highly recommend this book!"

Dr. David Allen
Dean of the School of Preaching
Southwestern Baptist Theological Seminary

www.ingramcontent.com/pod-product-compliance
Lightning Source LLC
Chambersburg PA
CBHW071438080526
44587CB00014B/1895